RAY GUY'S BEST

RAY GUY'S BEST

RAY GUY

An Atlantic Insight Book
Formac Publishing Company Limited
Halifax 1987

Canadian Cataloguing in Publication Data
Guy, Ray   Ray Guy's best
ISBN 0-88780-062-9
I. Title. PS8563.u9r39 1987   C818'.5402   C87-095108-4
PR9199.3.G89R39 1987

An Atlantic Insight Book

Formac Publishing Company Limited
5359 Inglis Street
Halifax, Nova Scotia
B3H 1J4
Printed and bound in Canada

CONTENTS

INTRODUCTION

Ray Guy has written a column in Atlantic Insight since its first issue in April, 1979. In a letter several years later, he recalled that debut and said the column had always been of special importance to him because, he wrote, "it allows me to proselytize the other side of the Cabot Strait where the need is great."

The column has, likewise, been of special importance to readers of Atlantic Insight — not as much for the proselytizing, as for the humour. Ray Guy's name is, of course, synonymous with humour but what makes his humour special is its edge of skepticism, its tempered cynicism, its remarkable compassion. He understands how the world works and how he and his fellow Newfoundlanders fit into it.

Often, he doesn't like what he sees; sometimes — paradoxically — that's when he's at his best. His writing has changed somewhat over the years — not only in style but in substance. The change reflects both the changing times and a reluctant maturity. Ray Guy still sees injustice and exploitation all around him but he sees them today with the satisfying attitude of one who can have an effect, of one who has a listening and respectful audience.

The columns in this collection represent work from each of the years since 1979. They've been chosen for their timelessness as well as for their readability. Whether you're reading them for the first time or as a longtime fan, we think you'll agree that these are, indeed, some of Ray Guy's Best.

Sharon Fraser
Editor
Atlantic Insight

OF
NEWFOUNDLAND
AND CANADA

OUR CLIMATE CONDEMNED US TO CANADA

It was our climate that gave Newfoundland Confederation with Canada. Plus polka dot rabbits.

We're unlike most other places. Some days in June and in January are interchangable. Winter lasts nine months followed by a milder spell which passes for the other three seasons. At least that's the way it is here in the southeast corner of the island. Nine months might seem like a harsh sentence. But what we mean by "winter" here is not a cut and dried thing. There's no head nor tail to it.

In other free Christian democracies you can set your calendar by the seasons. White Christmases are guaranteed. Promptly on the first day of spring the trees explode into leaf with a soft vegetable thunk. On midsummer's day, a heatwave arrives on time and at six minutes past four, September 21, every leaf unhitches itself simultaneously. Even in Newfoundland that's the sort of climate still being taught in the schools.

You get the same thing on calendars. Turn over to May and there's a picture of a maiden in national costume up to her armpits in tulips and apple blossoms in Ottawa or Vermont or Tweeney-Upon-Falstaff, Hants., Berks., Bucks., SW. 1, Eng. Press on to June and the summer heat is coming off the page in waves and the gin and quinine is being dispensed in the beeloud glades.

Here, however, the trees are just as bare on Coronation Day as they are at the Feast of the Circumcision while, on the other hand, there are shirtsleeve days in February and icebergs in July. Incest and poor diet have long been put forward to explain Newfoundland politics and Newfoundland politicians but, to my own mind at least, not enough weight has been given to climate. It's hard to be a warm, meaningful, sincere, relevant human being like they have in the States when, for nine months of the year, you may step out the door on green grass in the morning and come back to supper with the snow halfway up to the windowledges.

There are not many places on God's great globe, either, where you'll find polka dot rabbits. Normal, well-adjusted bunnies are brown in summer and white in winter. Ours bounce around in a quandary. They settle for nine months of mottled indecisiveness. The Newfoundland human being is in much the same cleft stick as the Newfoundland rabbit. For nine months of the year you wouldn't, if in your right senses, bet a five cent piece on what you're going to see when you look out the window the next morning.

Our weather forecasters mumble a lot. On TV, they go at their maps like windmills in a force 10 gale, interspersing all sorts of swoops and arrows with pregnant lice representing the sun and when they're finished I'll challenge anyone to repeat what they've just said. It saves them from being kicked to death in public. High-speed gibberish is their only method of self-defence in a place where a balmy and tranquil sunset can give way to a night like that on which Lucy Grey was lost.

Nature itself is befuddled by Newfoundland weather. Former ministers and their brothers-in-law know enough and can afford to hump off to Florida and stay there for the duration. But robin red breasts, for instance, can't decide when to migrate. Some of them never do. There's been one in my front yard the year round. It takes one step south and two north and manages to look bilious and confused at the same time — rather like Joe Clark trying to grasp the rudiments of Sri Lanka's fiscal policies. It looks ruffled and vexatious, as if it had been sucked through a vacuum cleaner. So do the people passing on the sidewalk. Newfoundland winter is a nine-month Screech hangover.

Our politics suffer thereby. Had Joey Smallwood's fellow delegates to Canada not been children of the Newfoundland climate when they went to Ottawa in the spring of 1948, we might not be labouring as we are today under the handicap of televised Canadian football, P. Trudeau and tinned B.C. salmon. Gordon Bradley, along with Smallwood and others, had been sent to Ottawa to make the final arrangements for Confederation. Gordon balked. Like our robin red breasts after Labour Day he was in two minds about the enterprise. But as chance would have it, the Newfoundland plenipotentiaries arrived in Ottawa in the midst of an early heat wave. Mr. Bradley was wearing that fleece-lined, cast-iron undergarment so necessary to survival in Newfoundland for much of the year. It was the custom among the older folk for the women to sew their men into these longjohns about the latter part of September and to cut them free again in early July.

In the heathenish malarial jungle of Ottawa in May, poor Gordon fell a victim to the heat and set his hand to those fatal terms of union on the promise that he be instantly whisked back to the blessed coolth of his natal isle. Our first Canadian senator, needless to say.

When it comes time to cut Canada adrift, let the deal be done in St. John's in May ... with the Ottawa chappies seated outside in their bathing drawers. It'd be all over in five minutes and they'd probably chuck in half Ontario as a going-away present.

COUNTRY COMFORT'S A PENTHOUSE IN THE CITY

When, in early days, there was a great cross-traffic of city mice visiting the country and country dittos going to the city, the done thing was for each group to dash back prematurely to its natal seat taking a sacred vow never to leave home again. In our granddads' time, the movement became one-sided as farm boys and girls flocked to town and stayed. But in the past decade or so, a large number of urbanites have either established themselves in the sticks or else tirelessly expressed a desire to do so.

Beauty is said to sometimes skip a generation or two and something like that must also happen to ancestral memories of chilblains, dunghills and kicks in the guts for squeezing old mooley-cows the wrong way. Somewhere along the line the rigours of country life are submerged in visions of bee-loud glades, prairie dawns and sleigh bells ring are ya listenin'. I doubt if there's a furniture showroom in the midst of Toronto that hasn't got a "painting" on the wall of a prairie sky, a Quebec farmhouse in the snow or fishing shacks sticking out of the Atlantic fog. Distance makes the heart grow fonder. Nostalgia-mongers do the grass back there worlds of good.

An aquaintance who was once given a mighty heave through a tavern doorway was at first inclined to caution that the landing itself had little or nothing to recommend it. But as time passed he tended to recall, instead, that the boost through the air was a rather exhilarating sensation. Time and distance also do odd things to rural memories.

My own first two decades were as rural as hell. The last two have been in St. John's, a place that's both fish and foul. It's not quite downtown Chicago but it does have pigeons, joggers and bedraggled old chaps on Water Street.

Newfoundlanders fall into two classes, those who are St. John's men and those who are not. Townies and baymen. You're stamped at birth and not even an appeal to the Queen's Mercy (either Buckingham Palace or the Pearly Gates) can change it. In fact, townies believe that the Queens of both England and Heaven are unfortunate baypersons. They believe that the old saw, "You can take the boy out of the bay but you can't take the bay out of the boy," is a heart-rending appeal for the Year of the Handicapped. And that if corrective surgery became available in Denmark all baymen would be off like shots.

To reinforce this chastely simple faith, they venture a few miles outside the city gates for a couple weeks each year to their "summer shacks" sprawled among the rocky crags beyond the suburbs like a huge misty Dogpatch. Here, they deliberately expose themselves to all the rustic horrors. Backfiring septic tanks, stinking camp stoves, attic wasps' nests, frothy-muzzled bulls with blood-stained horns, the silence of a dungeon and mattress-ticking on the TV.

Having had their annual purgative dose of "the bay" they toddle back to their bastion of enlightenment, civilization and bilious pigeons as fast as their weakened legs will carry them and prostrate themselves on the sidewalks of St. John's like some frazzled battalion of touring Pontiffs. Our townies believe that the country (or, in this case, "Out Around the Bay") is a place where, if you purchase a teacup, you have to put in a special order and wait six weeks for the saucer. Where the main manufacture is homespun wit, the raw materials for which must be imported. A pig-sticking, fish-gutting, snaggle-toothed, childbed-feverish place beyond the Pale, devoid of even gas station stickups and real, live cabinet ministers. Any of our townies who express an intention to go live in the country seldom make it across the city boundary line ahead of the little white loony wagon.

It may not be so cut and dried in other places. If you've spent 30 years hanging from a subway strap — close-packed from behind by a mass of garlicked, patchoulied, Holt-Renfrewed humanity and menaced in front by seated dozers who threaten to topple headfirst into your privates — braving blizzards to slop the hogs may look good.

Newfoundland has spawned few, if any, of its own back-to-the-earthers. Between the bogs and the rocks, there's precious little earth to go back to. Even in St. John's you can find, if not the simple, then all of the half-simple life you could possibly want.

The Maritimes is, I understand, chock-a-block with persons who've fled the hideous complications of urban living for double-shell houses, solar heating, airtight wood stoves, hydroponic gardens, windmill generators, ram-jets, composting crappers, airlocks, R-48, goat husbandry, hydraulic yogurt makers and half-finished submissions to *Harrowsmith.*

Most, I'll venture, come from Boston or Montreal rather than Moncton or Halifax. Your Haligonian, I dare say, is like your St. John's man, a true urban philosopher able to see eternity in a grain of sand, recapture the primitive thrill of the chase in sidewalk doggie-doo or the Great North woods in a potted geranium.

Some of this odd craving for "the country" found in other parts may be a residue from the past when we were expected to do our best to ape our betters. The better classes doted on "the country," which was not your rain-sodden picnic bench in Fundy or Gros Morne but rustic cottages like Blenheim or Castle Howard or Vanderbilt's "The Breakers."

Roughing it meant squads of footmen dispatched at a double trot to unroll Wilton carpets by the margin of an artificial lake, followed by a heavy brigade of other retainers staggering under champagne and roast partridges. Those able to re-create this to their own satisfaction in a gravel pit off the Trans-Canada Highway in the company of three howling kiddies, a bitching spouse and mosquitoes robust enough to drown out 109 portable tape recorders are either truly blessed or else well around the twist.

Meanwhile, ensconce me in a Toronto penthouse with room service and all mod cons and I'll monger you reams of rustic nostalgia until the cows come home and the chickens to roost at the 28th storey.

SEE DICK AND JANE RUN. SEE LUCY BITE THE DUST

Lately, in an elevator in Toronto, I overheard two British Columbian women trying to top one another regarding the simplicity and therefore the virtue of the private schools in which they had installed their offspring. I mentioned this partly to reassure Mother once again that even though I never made it to brain surgeon, the life of a freelance journalist is a glamourous and useful one which takes me to exotic spots. One of the B.C. ladies boasted that her kinder went to a place so sensible and sound that they were taught nothing but Greek, Latin, English and arithmetic ... none of this new math or how to supercharge your tricycle. The other said that *her* tots went to a place so advanced that it used no English literature texts printed after 1912.

They got off the Otis six floors below mine so I was left to speculate that in one place the bootlaces of the little scholars were tied in hard knots to prevent them counting above 10 while in the other the infants were given slabs of granite and chisels to chip out uplifting bits of Homer.

Educational methods are changing all the time. I started off down the pathways of organized enlightenment in the company of Jerry and Jane and their alsatian, yclept Laddie. Jerry and Jane were in a constant state of amazement at the way Laddie was able to walk, run and, when put to it, even jump. By page 18, Laddie chased a squirrel. We had to learn to spell the name of Laddie's quarry. Since there are no squirrels in Newfoundland it was obviously early preparation for a job on the mainland. Jerry and Jane went to something called kindergarten so we had to learn how to spell that, too. Kindergarten was something they had up there in the States. We went to "primer class" to learn such things as how to spell kindergarten.

By the age of five I knew that "the red light says stop; the green light says go" but was well into puberty before I actually got to St. John's and saw what was then possibly the only traffic light in Newfoundland. It was located, I think, at a junction called Rawlin's Cross. Which brings us to the denominational system of education here.

There used to be separate schools for Church of Englanders, Wesleyans, Roman Catholics, Salvationists, Pentecostalists and Seventh Day Adventists. Except for the Papists and the Pents, the rest have pretty much amalgamated now. But back to Rawlin's Cross called, for short, The Cross. A person named (why not?) Paddy Murphy lived between two shopkeepers at Rawlin's Cross who were both notorious for their sharp practices. He eventually died and soon hereafter when Father Power was quizzing a class on spiritual matters he asked: "Joseph White, my lad, tell us who it was that died on the Cross between two thieves."

"Paddy Murphy, Father."

Jerry and Jane eventually gave place to Dick and Jane, and their dog was a cocker spaniel named Spot. He was every bit as agile as Laddie which brought forth constant exclamations from Dick and Jane. In Catholic schools, though, Spot was the canine prodigy of David and Anne. David's and Anne's kindergarten had a crucifix above the blackboard and a Bride of Christ to teach them such spiffy conversational gambits as "Oh, oh, oh. Look, look, look. See Spot run."

My parents and their contemporaries made do with Tom. He, too, had a dog but it was apparently nameless ... "This is Tom. This is Tom's dog. Tom eats two eggs a day. See how fat he is." But that generation had the advantage of "Royal Readers." The dogs of Dick and Jane and David and Anne were put far behind them before the first school year was out.

Instead of grades, you were classed by the book number. St. John's men, to demonstrate their sophistication compared to the rest of the human race, still snicker at the baymen who went into a shoe shop on Water Street and said: "Give us a pair of boots to fit a girl in Number Five Book."

There was none of this Dick and Jane pap in the Royal Readers. Life was real and life was earnest. In Number Three Book alone there are upward of a dozen hideous juvenile deaths. These kiddies copped it either in the course of excruciatingly noble acts or while disobeying their elders and betters. Sometimes both. Take the sad but inspirational case of the brothers, Robert and James, who climbed up some scaffolding to a church roof — which they ought not to have done — and fell off. Robert clutched a beam and James managed to grab Robert's legs. "In this awful position the lads hung, shouting for help. At last the strain of the double weight became more than Robert's hands could bear. 'Could you save yourself if I let go?' asked James. 'Then good-bye and God bless you!' cried the noble boy as he let go his hold and ... "

Thereafter, we may suppose, Robert walked through life radiating repentance and gratitude, his knuckles grazing the pavement.

You can still count on the older race to come indoors out of a blizzard and say, "Christ, this is worse than the night Lucy Gray was lost!" This Lucy ("the sweetest thing that ever grew inside a human door!" no less) was sent off with a lantern to fetch Mummy from town while Daddy stayed home and "raised his hook and snapped a fagot-band" — either an interesting perversion, I suppose, or an archaic cottage industry. They traced her little footprints through the snow but they disappeared in the middle of the bridge. Hide nor hair was ever found of her although we were told in stanza 15 that "some maintain that to this day she is a living child" which is an odd conclusion as it would put her well up into her 90s.

Number Three Book has some general information, too. "The Tongue," for instance. "What a wonderful thing our tongue is! No other part of our body moves so freely. It can be thrust out and pulled back very quickly; and it may be moved from side to side, or up and down, at pleasure."

Whenever I reread this scientific treatise I get, for some reason, an image of Lucy Gray being thus enlightened while sitting on Lewis Carroll's knee.

But the heft of the Royal Readers is how to perish with a stiff upper lip. Not a bad course of instruction at a time when there were two world wars yet to come. Lucy Gray and Robert the orangutan point the way.

OUR POLITICIANS PLUNDER. WE LIKE THEM THAT WAY

A St. John's radio chat show recently ran a poll on the status of politicians in local society. I believe they ran a notch ahead of child molesters but gave considerable ground to grave robbers and pussy cat garrotters. We prefer them that way.

In Newfoundland, politics is one thing and government is another. Here in the land of the rising scum, a politician is someone who, once all his relatives have been sated, shares some of his plunder of "The Gum'mint" purse with his constituents. "The Gum'mint," on the other hand, is a demi-divine creation composed vaguely of royal governors, the Church and the better classes of St. John's. It has nothing to do with the price of trimmed navel beef or potholes in the roads. Once it was used to issue postage stamps and hang people, but it doesn't even do that any more.

A long history of colonial rule, an interval of quasi self-government, 16 years (1933-1949) of government by appointed commission followed by Smallwood provided no firm grounding in civics. Perhaps the closest we get to a concept of "The Gum'mint" is like the one in E.J. Pratt's epic of the scrimmage between the whale and the giant squid. You know the two brutes are down there somewhere in the depths locked in mortal combat but you're not about to go down there and referee the match. No more than you would dream of concerning yourself with the mighty submarine plungings and thrashings of "The Gum'mint."

At certain intervals the two monstrous combatants heave themselves up into the daylight to crash out of sight again beneath the waves. It is one of the most thrilling sights in nature.

It's called an election. During the brief interval in which God's ferocious handiwork presents itself to human view you place your bet on the monster that seems to be getting the upper hand. This is called voting. To ensure that the Tory leviathan and the Liberal kraken don't rise too close and upset your dory you pour a constant stream of tribute money into the mysterious deeps. This is called paying taxes. It works like a charm. That's pretty well "The Gum'mint." Politicians may be like the barnacles, limpets and sea lice sticking to the great carcasses, but that's about the only perceived connection.

This peculiar blind spot makes our merry band of legislators the happiest and luckiest dogs in creation. True, they're considered the lowest of breeds but they're actually *expected* to be rogues, pilferers and artful dodgers. "They're all alike!" is the cheerful description of politicians you'll get from most Newfoundlanders. All pots calling kettles black and the other way around. How came this unique outlook?

In 1933 when Newfoundland went bankrupt and all semblance of democratic government was suspended, a royal commission was set up by the dear old mother country to see what the bloody hell had been going on here. There'd been political corruption on a grand scale. The national budget hadn't been balanced in 12 years and the civil service was compared to the Mexican army: "Very little pay but unlimited licence to loot." The prime minister escaped a howling mob by scuttling over a back fence. One of his acolytes was, need it be said, the young Joey Smallwood. My Lords Commissioners, when they started rooting around in the shambles, were aghast.

Why was it, they asked, that in Newfoundland politics the sediment always rose to the top? An answer was that the Newfoundland public doted on political skullduggers. If your honourable member was a dab hand at lining his own pockets it was a fair bet he'd be just as agile at plundering the public purse on behalf of his loyal constituents. Or, rather, "The Gum'mint" purse, a mysterious fountain with no visible plumbing connection to taxation. After 1949, federal largesse from Ottawa boosted this odd concept of government into the rosiest of clouds. And so, by the maxim that people get exactly the kind of government they deserve, all Newfoundlanders were condemned as rogues and scoundrels.

There's pitifully little to disprove this nasty notion. Several times during the 23-year reign of Joey Smallwood, even he feared it might be necessary to appoint an opposition since only three or four warm bodies had been elected to it. Smallwood came to us with Canadian goodies and the operating manual bequeathed to him by that prime minister, one of his idols, who'd skedaddled over the back fence. He was followed by Moores who found the Smallwoodian formula too seductively workable to pitch out. With a great flourish, Moores brought in corrective legislation but a recent royal commission discovered the obvious — as generalissimo of the northern branch of the Mexican army, Moores had in some ways topped Smallwood.

Those who'd hoped for some political novelty to brighten their golden years had them dashed by the coming of Peckford. He's an almost perfect Smallwood clone. With another election in the wind, it would curdle your vital juices to hear young Alfie toss off implications of great new industries and pies in the sky.

When, in 1949, Newfoundland ceased to be even a semblance of a nation some fellow at the ceremonies in the ballroom of the Newfoundland Hotel cried out (for, by golly, though stupid we are passionate little buggerinos): "God help thee, Newfoundland!" The departing royal governor was heard to sniff: "God helps those who help themselves."

There's another election in the wind, but no hopes are held for a first-class spectacle. The Liberal squid has most of its tentacles in splints and can do little but squirt while the Tory whale has become so bloated it can barely heave its blubber against a mild tide.

Pity us, with not even a half-decent show to lighten our predicament. But what sympathy can we expect from you bunch west of the Cabot Strait who've done your best to ruin the only industry we had going here — bilking the feds. Your milk of human kindness must have turned to plain yogurt; otherwise you would not have started sending scoundrels to Ottawa who can run rings around our rogues.

LET'S HEAR IT FOR ST. JOHN'S TAVERNS

U nlike myself, one of my grandfathers used to frequent the nefarious and multitudinous taverns of St. John's but once a year. For all that, he died in mid-life on the eve of the Great War. Grandaddy used to come to St. John's at the end of March to make the rounds of the public houses. He did so to recruit the 15 or 20 willing workers needed to plough and fish for him until the end of October.

This was serious and crucial work. I'm unable to say that my maternal grandpa ever tippled on his annual rounds or ever, in consequence, sat in a St. John's gutter with a contented grin on his face; because he died young and was therefore enlarged and sainted in death beyond what he probably was in life.

St. John's taverns are a touchy subject, anyway.

It is generally better for your liver if you stay out of them altogether and for your health in general if you never mention those public houses by name in the public prints.

There's a mystery and an aura of menace attached to St. John's taverns. Always has been since the days when Captain Cook and Captain Henry Morgan (the fellow on the rum bottle) sat in them. It was less than five years ago that 13 of them took fire and burned down within a twelvemonth — and not a word of explanation to this day. The first Newfoundland parliament sat in a St. John's tavern. It set the tone for parliaments here since. The landlady threw the legislators out into the road for non-payment of rent and bar tabs. She confiscated the mace and held it until the blighters paid up.

A recent premier and several of his ministers kept one of them open five hours after legal closing time with a bluff and straightforward statement to the proprietor concerning the side his bread was buttered on — and then rollicked up the main aisle of the Basilica in time for early Good Friday service. Not long before that a citizen had taken the Liberal party to court, waving around cancelled cheques and other facts and figures while protesting that his contribution to the cause hadn't got him his promised tavern licence.

A licence to operate a tavern in St. John's is still much preferred to a seat in the Canadian Senate. Elsewhere, things might go better with Coke but in St. John's, politics is the favourite mix with booze.

Our first provincial government and premier were Liberal because (as Joey Smallwood tells it) Jack Pickersgill showed him the national party's list of benefactors and the figure for Seagram's alone had much the same effect on Joey as the latest reports from Hibernia have on Brian Peckford. One of Mr. Smallwood's trips to court on points of civic indiscretion concerned some hootch shops being rented to the government by a company which included himself, at rates per square foot much, much above average.

In Captain Cook's day, every sixth building along Water Street was a tavern and rum drunk per capita was 50 gallons a year. These glory days are now being approached once again. Young lawyers, doctors and/or dope peddlers have revived the ancient custom with a relish. Since the purge by fire a few years ago, new taverns have sprung up in downtown St. John's with befuddling rapidity. Plastic and boutiquey, most of them, and there's the outrageous possibility that even Georges Street, once the bootleg capital of Newfoundland, will soon support a Trader Vic's.

But old hands stick with their old favourites. One of mine went nameless for six months because a prissy city council wouldn't allow it to call itself "Dirty Dick's" — in Newfoundland, another term for an unhygienic phallus. It was there that I was privileged to watch one of the biggest real estate developers in Canada slowly slide off the can and doze blissfully on the floor of the convenience with his bare bottom sticking up in the air, and where, to my eternal shame as a newspaper reporter, successful plans to import pot by the ton were discussed night after night and me too naive to know what it was I was overhearing.

"Dirty Dick's" no longer exists so it's one name I feel free to mention without getting my kneecaps Black and Deckered. Almost. St. John's taverns have always had a way of undoing poor unsophisticated baymen like myself.

One of the few places in town where we felt safe had a sign on the door:"Outport Ladies and Gentlemen Welcome. Proper Dress Required. This Means Necktie." But it, too, has disappeared and with it the 78-year-old outport gentleman who once entered wearing only a neckpiece to test the minimum dress requirements.

Rather than darken some of these St. John's dens of iniquity, many baymen stuck to Jakey's Gin which was a brand of aftershave lotion named after the man who flogged it by the hogshead and who rose to the lower ranks of St. John's mercantilism long before marijuana wholesaling or a law degree became the entry ticket.

But my grandaddy would no longer recognize St. John's taverns. I sure as hell don't. They've recently added saki for the benefit of international travellers and Tennent's beer for the sake of oil rig workers fresh from the North Sea.

And yes, there are already things called fern bars.

PLAYING THE NEWF GOOF FOR MAINLAND MEDIA

"They tell me you're the funny guy around here," said the chap from CBC *National*, "so all I want from you is a short, snappy comment on each of the three political leaders." It isn't easy being a stock flutter in the regional pulse. Mainland newspaper and television "teams" divebomb you in relays demanding you make plain to them the mysterious east in 250 words or less, fuelled by a maximum of only two beers. These chaps are invariably harried. They have exactly a day and a half. Then it's off again to stuff northern Saskatchewan into a nutshell. A fogged-in airport is the constant hag that rides them.

Luckily, they know just what it is they want: (1) an up-and-coming young leftish person destined to loom large in Newfoundland's future; (2) an up-and-coming young rightish person, likewise destined; (3) horny-handed fisherfolk in a picturesque village no more than 20 miles from St. John's airport; (4) a woman sociologist from the university, preferably one who rears goats and operates an airtight, cast-iron, wood-burning apparatus; (5) a populist buffoon who, with the fisherfolk, counterbalances the profundities of the two up-and-comings and the goat lady.

It seems straightforward. All our mainland press have to do is dash through the five categories and collect the standard offering from each. To make things even simpler, the same person holds office under each heading for a term of five years. Richard Cashin, the fisherman's union chap, occupies category Number One while Miller Ayre, a businessman and St. John's city councillor, fills Number Two. Number Three is staffed by three or four fishermen in Petty Harbour, a village conveniently near St. John's but which looks like Peggy's Cove, N.S. did when Peggy was still a maiden. In the fourth category, there are actually two women sociologists. They divide the burden, depending on whose goat herd is due to freshen. I have the honour to hold down the fifth posting myself with my term still a year and a half to run.

An easy 36 hours work — or so you might think — to pop off a plane, make the rounds and head back to Toronto with the socio-economic essence of Newfoundland safely in the can. But in Newfoundland, alas, things are never that simple. A flat tire gets much flatter here than it does in central Canada and it's likely to stay flat for five hours longer. There are other hindrances. A Toronto reporter once told me he could encapsulate the whole of Manitoba and Northern Ontario in less time than it took him to do Newfoundland.

The CBC chap confided that those horny-handed, weather-beaten, fisherfolk in Petty Harbour have become so professional they're almost useless. That's understandable. By now, they must have more camera time under their belts than most ACTRA members. The very gulls have learned to swoop past on cue. "I was tempted to tell them," sighed the CBC chap, "to drop their phoney Newfie act and show us something of their souls."

"Lucky you didn't," I said. "They might have misunderstood you and, instead of their souls, you could have had a haddock wrapped around your ears."

The script that category Number Three has by now honed to perfection is to the effect that "Far as we're concerned, bye, every one of them jeezly politicians in there to St. John's and up there in Ottawa should be in hell's fiery flames with their backs broke." But that's out of date now. What's wanted is less rustic pique and more salt-of-the-earth reassurances that This Great Nation of Ours stands firm even in the easternmost nooks; a script well-sprinkled with chunks of soul; a solid rehearsal in what the mainland media regard as a Newfie accent (thick enough to slice but just a notch this side of requiring subtitles); and an indoor set with stuffed kittiwakes on strings.

In fact, we all need to pull up our socks and get our acts together. We need a shared appointments secretary, a scale of fees and a kiosk in St. John's airport. Those two young up-and-comings are often up and gone on holiday in the Antilles just when mainland media teams need them most desperately. The lady sociologists spend too much time mucking around with their goats, the horny-handed weatherbeatens are still struggling with outdated scripts and the populist buffoon ... Ready for retirement. I knew it was high time to relinquish office when I saw the disappointment on the face of the CBC *National* fellow. All he wanted was a snappy comment on each of the three political leaders.

I couldn't come through. It was a poor excuse that I had a broken leg still a-mending, a six-month-old upstairs with a rising fever, a Block man at the kitchen table shaking his head over my income-tax returns and the upshot of a recent breathalyzer test still pending. The CBC was welcome to my blood but you couldn't see my merry old soul for bandages.

UNITY GARBAGE IS CANADIAN GARBAGE

As he trudged up Parliament Hill in 1949 to help sign New-foundland over to Canada, Joey Smallwood was asked how he felt. "Much the same way," he imagined, "that a prime minister of Canada will feel on the day he takes a similar walk up Capitol Hill in Washington."

No flies on Joe.

He had firmly pegged the prospects for Canadian unity even as he checked his breast pocket to make sure he'd brought his notes, notes for a speech exhorting Newfoundlanders to drop to their knees and cry thanksgiving to God for the everlasting benefits of Confederation. We don't pound our pillows and chew the corners of our sheets as much as some other Canadians think we should. We get reproachful glances even in places like Halifax where we would have expected a modicum of empathy.

I once sat at lunch next to a pleasant, blue-rinsed Haligonian who said, "You Newfoundlanders, of all people, must be terribly concerned about Canadian unity. After all, look what Canada has given you."

"We don't give a beaver's dam," I, of all people, replied. "We can always auction ourselves off between the Russians and the States, or hook up with St. Pierre and Miquelon, or declare the republic and colonize the Canadian scraps."

This blasphemy kicked her pacemaker into overdrive. I expected poached salmon in the kisser. You don't kid around about other people's sacred phobias. In this case, what appears to be Newfoundland indifference is put down to cold-bloodedness, cynicism or, of course, stupidity. Maybe so, but it'll take more to raise us from error and get our drawers into patriotic Canadian knots than forced Canada Day hoopla and the frantic fluttering of Maple Leaf flags. By the way, wouldn't a rhubarb leaf have been the better choice?

From my smattering of Canadian history I seem to recall that in the beginning, the Brits stuck maple leaves in their hats so they could creep closer and puncture the Frenchies. Would you salute something that guys who put a musket ball through your great-great-grandaddy's brisket once hid behind?

Anyway, the unity circus strikes us here as being so heavy-handed it stinks of desperation. But we mustn't put on airs. I understand there were snickers in other parts of Canada, too, when the purpose-crafted "Life of Tom Thomson" appeared on television. "It may be garbage Tom," cried one of the mackinawed visionaries waving a freshly done canvas, "but, by God, at least it's Canadian garbage."

I recently saw something similar in the works on Water Street near the foot of Signal Hill. A unity film crew had hired five local youngsters to raise their little fists and cry "Yaaaay Canadaaaa!" in unison. There were hitches. A drunk slumped out of a nearby tavern and peed against a pole. A gang of the tot actors' contemporaries swooped through on tricycles lisping rude words. Unpatriotic fog rolled in and blotted out Signal Hill.

Late in the day the cameraman darted into a store and came back with six packs of Cheesies. He stapled these to a board and, at the crucial moment, flashed them at the kiddies. Their faces lit up with a facsimile of Canadian zeal, but what half of them shouted was, "Yaaaay Cheesies!"

"Hard work, old man?" I asked the director.

"Naaa," he shrugged. "Compared to beer commercials, it's a piece of cake."

When it comes to Confederation, we're a bit like Napoleon's mother. Madame Mère gloomed about the palace for years muttering, "Yes, but will it last?" And, like that wiry old Corsican dame, Newfoundland may be the least surprised or discommoded if Canada collapses. At a plant nursery you pay more for a tree that's already been transplanted several times. Its roots are stronger and more compact. It is better able to withstand shock and, in more than 400 years, Newfoundland has been uprooted as often as a front-yard dandelion.

We have been, in our time, an English colony, an island divided between England and France, an English colony (except for St. Pierre and Miquelon) again, a quasi-independent nation, a dictatorship ruled by a secret commission, a fiefdom of the U.S. military and, latterly, a Canadian province. We've been through the ropes, and it takes more than a pack of Cheesies to make our eyes bright.

Others, to the westward, may be right to scramble to the barricades, leap off the Niagara Escarpment or swallow garbage as long as it's Canadian. We fail to see the advantages. If that's stupidity, it comes from a history in which, no matter what was done to us, as long as we called ourselves Newfoundlanders there was always a Newfoundland. To me, that seems less like stupidity and more like justifiable arrogance.

AH, THE NEVER FADING CHARM OF BUNG HOLE TICKLE

In the whole catalogue of charm-ridden Atlantic villages so celebrated in song, story and regional magazine article, none stands closer to my own heart than Bung Hole Tickle on the wave-laved shores of G.D. Bay.

It was some years ago on one of those perfect late-June days that I stumbled upon this sequestered hamlet and the magic realism of that moment would have taxed the brush of a Pratt (Chris, not Mary) or of a Colville. Many times since I have found myself drawn back to Bung Hole Tickle and never has its soul-soothing tranquillity failed to work its wonder on me. (Jet trails and asphalt highways have destroyed much of Newfoundland's precious, bucolic heritage yet B.H. Tickle clings to its isolation and is often confused by the postal service with such well-known centres of population here as Leading Tickles and Piper's Hole.)

It was the merciless big-city grind that first drove me blindly into that G.D. Bay haven. For all its veneer of suave, swinging sophisication, St. John's can also be granite-hard on those who seek of life the kind, the gentle, the meaningful, the puerile. Early on that late-June day I'd had an argument with my hard-nosed city editor. He'd accused me of writing an article, in exchange for $20 and a bottle of Johnnie Walker, favourable to a shopping mall developer who'd proposed erecting over the Mary Queen of Peace Cemetery. I'd, in turn, explained to him that he was a dirty Mick and where else had he got that new chesterfield suite if not in return for all those editorials promoting the second Papist lieutenant-governor in succession ... an unspeakable breach of custom here.

And so it was that I still spat teeth and blood, not much mollified by the few quick knees I'd been able to get in, as my motor car crested a hill and I suddenly came face to face with that gem of rustic serenity known as Bung Hole Tickle.

Wheeling gulls scribed peace on the blue vault and white terns fluttered and dipped in the ultramarine cup below. I stopped my car and strolled over to a low roadside knoll the better to take it all in. Also, as it had been a three-hour drive, to let it all out. Just then, from a dozen feet below, came a voice. It belonged to a sun-blessed, tow-headed child of 10 or 12 years of age who sat on a rock playing intently with some toy or other in its lap.

"Arrr, go fugg 'ee seff!" chirped the child in so pure an 18th-century Devonshire accent as it has been my privilege to hear in Newfoundland.

"And good day to you, too, my little man," I replied. "Tell me, do I see a village fête in progress down there in what is presumably your natal seat?"

The child repeated its earlier greeting and added several other archaic endearments. I wished the little tyke likewise and set off down the narrow road toward a green near the beach where the villagers had assembled in midsummer revelry.

Snatching up my Nikon I skipped from my motor and approached the tableau. An elderly lady with indifferent dental work was being in some way honoured. She reclined against a stout post while her neighbours laid tributes of kindling and dry brush at her feet.

Just then a rock a little larger than a gannet's egg glanced off my left temple and as I heard my windshield go a moment later I had the grace to blush. What business had I, a big-city slicker, to intrude on these simple folk unannounced and uninvited. Shamed, I drove quickly back up the hill even as smoke commenced to rise from their festal fire.

Yet, in the weeks and months ahead, my thoughts turned again and again to Bung Hole Tickle especially whenever the big-city grind threatened to get me down or the malevolence of the city editor weighed heavily upon me.

It was then I had the fortune to meet Professor Tory Archibald of the University, possibly the greatest authority on charm-ridden Atlantic villages we have.

From conversations with Dr. Archibald and with the great and good friends I made in Bung Hole Tickle as the strange bonds between it and me grew ever stronger, a full picture of that spikier Brigadoon emerged.

"Bung Hole, of course, from the orifice of a cask refers to the narrow entrance to that cove," explained Dr. Archibald, "whilst 'tickle,' a shallow, tide-rippled passage between island and mainland would also apply here."

So far as is known, the first inhabitants, five brothers and a sister of the Sunks family of Poole, England, established the community in the mid-1700s. The records are sketchy. In some versions the Sunkses emigrated hastily after charges of sheep-stealing had been levelled; in others, deportation followed on rumours of interference with said livestock.

At any rate, the six Sunkses appeared to have lived, multiplied and perished peacefully and uneventfully for the next 100 years or so in the little community they had carved from the wilderness. The first census of 1856 reports that 18 Sunks families and, inexplicably, three families named Boggs were domiciled in Bung Hole Tickle together with their goods, chattels, "manifold sheep of inferior quality and an lyttle black fellow captured off an American frigate."

"The genetic pool there has never been much larger than your average pudding basin," Dr. Archibald said, "but therein lies the charm of the place, don't you think?"

Not much else is recorded in the annals of Bung Hole Tickle until 1912 when a religious upheaval of sorts occurred. The little church is located on a bluff above the village so as to have a clear view of The Godsend Sunkers, a treacherous reef which has sent many a salvageable vessel to her doom.

In 1912, Bung Hole Tickle was under the pastoral charge of one Rev. Job Bales. When news of the *Titanic* disaster reached the village there were mutterings against Rev. Bales, and his theology was questioned. He later arrived in St. John's with both

Achilles tendons cut and, after managing for some years a tattoo parlour on the seedier (if possible) end of Duckworth Street passed completely from the fabric of St. John's society.

"Arrr, bye, me grandpap told me 'ee war droonk as per usual and fell agin' a brandy bottle," a village friend has told me. "Eee war no man of God. We had a puffitly good iceberg lyin' that same night not one mile off the Tickle yonder ... so where war she if Bales had good connection with He?"

Days come, days go, winters change to springs and springs to what passes for summers yet Bung Hole Tickle changes not. The womenfolk sit and gossip by their cottage doors in all seasons; the menfolk mull over the situation in Afghanistan or San Salvador and tend their sheep; the young ones are scarce.

For in the early years of the Smallwood era some overly-keen social worker convinced the menfolk that a vasectomy was part of the ritual connection with joining the Orange Lodge.

"A precious rustic backwater, no doubt about it," concludes the good Professor Archibald. "Still, we mustn't let Newfie chauvinism blind us here. Nova Scotia and New Brunswick boast as good or better having the advantage of the Scottish and the French influences, don't you see."

Nonetheless, it's Bung Hole Tickle for me, bye!

PLUNGE INTO PINEAPPLE PLANTATION, MAUDE

S omewhere east of Eden the Lord God planted a garden, but the inhabitants of Newfoundland and Labrador have long been assured that theirs is the land He gave to Cain.

Paradise is too good for the likes of us. For instance, there used to be two Paradises in Placentia Bay — Great Paradise and Little Paradise — but the Smallwood administration resettled the inhabitants and sent a federal agent with a flaming sword to bar their return. And there's a town of Paradise within 16 km of St. John's, but it is classified as a Local Improvement District, so it's a safe bet that the chap with the tail has already clued those folk in on the knowledge of good and evil.

Yet horticulturalists here, while they may sometimes falter, never despair. The official line is that they are harmless lunatics in a class with NDP organizers or tourists to Moncton. Soil, they are told, doesn't exist because the last glaciers pushed it all into the ocean to form the Grand Banks, except for 127 bushels remaining in the Codroy Valley.

But we gardeners soldier on though the plot be rocky and the imported expertise confusing. For example, English gardening books advise setting out your peas in February (when we still have four feet of snow), and American texts warn that lupins languish on this side of the ocean (yet they grow like weeds by Newfoundland highways).

One of the few encouragements we get from the greater world is a thing called the "Canadian Plant Hardiness Zone Map," which divides the nation into swirling, coloured bands numbered from zero to nine. Nine occurs only in tiny pockets on the B.C. coast. It has only light frost and jolly little of it. The best Newfoundland can do is a narrow band of six. But that is far better than we'd been led to believe. Quebec and New Brunswick don't rise above a five. Ontario has got a small bit of six between Toronto and Windsor, Nova Scotia has got some and so does P.E.I. That's all the six there is in Canada until you get to British Columbia.

Newfoundland may never become the watermelon capital of North America, but neither are we the howling tundra. Hardiness zones aren't everything, of course. Soil, shelter, sun and protective snow cover also mean a lot. I recall my surprise outside a hotel in Grand Falls (zone four) when I found myself up to the hips in lavender. An unwholesome awe of English gardening texts and a certain local inferiority complex had said it wasn't possible.

Now, it would be grapes of the sourest kind to say that Victoria, B.C., doesn't have a slight horticultural edge on the Atlantic provinces. But it isn't Paradise. Bald rock sticks up everywhere in that city, and except in spots of constant irrigation, her lawns in high summer are the color of a camelhair coat. Our grass, in the middle of August, stays a blazing green and is as juicy as rhubarb stalks. But no one place has everything. Let us keen amateur horticulturalists be guided by Lord Aberconway. Who he? An old port-and-cigars personage, I fancy, without whose Forewords precious few English garden books slip by to the printers. And what says the great Lord Aberconway to the neophyte who has crept humbly to his knee to hear distilled in plain words the essence of what the greatest gardening nation in the world has to pass on? "Find out what you can grow well and grow lots of it, don't y'know! Harrump!" A lesson to us all, me lord. As in so many other areas, that cursed Newfoundland inferiority complex still has a filthy grip. There are scattered examples of what can be grown here and they are constantly before our eyes, but there's no general rush to proceed past potatoes and petunias. There's that lavender hedge in Grand Falls, for instance, and 15-foot rhododendrons in Bowring Park, and holly bushes to the eaves of a few houses around St. John's, or the 12-foot hollyhocks in Corner Brook or the apple, pear, cherry, plum and apricot orchard in Notre Dame Bay (zone four!). There's heather and lupins and foxgloves growing wild. Spring is late and you can't risk much in the ground outside before Empire Day, but the simple cure is a few sticks and a piece of plastic sheet, and we may smile at the Niagara Peninsula. On the other hand, winter is also tardy, and one rare year I and many others brought acceptable bunches of roses from the garden to the Christmas dining table.

We are constantly selling our little acre short. I was surprised to learn that 25% of P.E.I.'s agricultural produce is accounted for by — tobacco! If there, then surely here.

And if tobacco then surely barley-corn, and so provisioned we may smack our posteriors at those bloodsucking parasites at Revenue Canada and their Sintax. Magic mushrooms are another thing. Magic mushrooms, as you may recall, came into the news a few years ago when the younger set became uncommonly frisky in the meadows of Vancouver Island. Typical of Lotus Land, we sniffed, where anything'll grow and where anything that grows will be tried once.

Last summer, the constables at Grand Falls, the lavender capital of Newfoundland, raised the alarm that maggotty-headed young layabouts there had discovered that we had magic mushrooms, too, and were rapidly turning themselves into depraved, anti-social, drug-crazed gas-bar attendants.

A sad day for society but a glorious one for horticulture. Pineapples in Pooch Cove next? Sugar cane in Seldom Come By? Frangipani in Fortune? And we thought turnips were the most we could manage here on the Arctic rim. By the way, the lotus, or your Nelumbo nucifera, can be brought along quite nicely in many parts of Newfoundland if the roots are brought into a cellar for winter, and I have had calla lilies overwinter outside for four years now here in St. John's.

This, need it be said, is all novelty and experimentation, but it is a tremendously stimulating exercise, amusing and not without its virtue. For how dull would be the gardens of England herself had not those remarkable Victorians brought back the plants of the world to her shores, where they were tested in a buoyant spirit of almost childlike curiosity. They rode their hobby horses up to glorious peaks.

I doubt that St. John's corn will ever equal Fredericton's or that our Avondale will ever challenge the Annapolis Valley or that the Great Northern Peninsula will ever support a first class viticulture. The point is that we are not a bald rock whose soil was swept away 15,000 years ago to feed the fishes. We are a temperate place with many advantages but populated by timid gardeners.

So plunge into the garden, Maude, bring that mould to good tilth, dung well each steaming plot, "go bind thou up yon dangling apricocks," find out what we can grow well and let's grow lots of it.

Me? Well, actually, at this time of year I find that my back goes out and that, according to the best medical advice, I'm better off indoors on the couch with a glass of California plonk watching *Three's Company* reruns. To you, I pass, with failing back, the torch.

WHAT, BE JAYSUS, IS THE ONE AND TRUE IMAGE OF NEWFOUNDLAND?

Are you happy?"
"Happy as a lamb on a headstone."
Here was a Newfie who disremembered completely the pinnacle of contentment said to be achieved only by a swine in excrement. This Newfie was on national television. Or, at least, he was a Canadian actor playing a Newfie in an old people's home in Toronto.

Newfie John and his girlfriend had won at bingo. When Newfies win at anything they do the obvious. They spend it all as soon as possible while leaving a trail of quaint sayings in their wake.

This geezer hired a big car and driver and went to Niagara Falls. And, be Jaysus, didn't the ice in the river put him in mind of the times he went down to the Labrador in a schooner? Yes, be Jaysus, it was bound to!

Bound, also, to make him as happy as a lamb on a headstone. Supposing he received a copy of the Dictionary of New-foundland English for Christmas and supposing the show (*All the Days of My Life*) is a series, he'll be back with more of the same.

Newfies on national television are as scarce as lambs on headstones. One of the few I can remember is Gordon Pinsent as a witch on *The Beachcombers*. Within 28 minutes he came up with three quaint sayings and his CBC-Newfie accent — Irish-Australian-Devonshire minus bottom dentures — never slipped from start to finish.

There'll be much more of the same. The pay is adequate. But doing bits for overseas consumption about a parochial, inbred, pinched and navel-gazing dump like Newfoundland can be hazardous to your health. I know.

Imagewise, sweetheart, this place is schizophrenic. Some of us don't give three sucks of a bitter lemon if we're called Newfies or not. Others react as if granny'd been disinterred and shipped off to a travelling freak show in Algeria.

We have here both the fiddle faction and the anti-fiddle faction; the "Kill-a-Whitecoat-for-Christ" brigade and the "Slugging-Seals-Is-Some-Outre" contingent; the "Precious Heritage" crowd and the "Pink-TB-Spits-Was-the-Pits" gang.

As long as this dissension about the one and true image of Newfoundland is kept local the towrow stays at a dull roar. Flung dung and tooth and claw are the accepted weapons and the number of actual homicides is hardly worth talking about. It is only when any Newfoundlander ventures any view of Newfoundland for the consumption of the greater world that hell cracks and the devil pops out.

Regardless of class, creed, colour or religion, the rest of the population unites in full fury against the mortal sinner. It's 526,847 against you and your mom. Every Newfie becomes an Un-Newfie Activities Committee of one.

This state of affairs can drive international communicators like the CBC out of their little tiny skulls. Last New Year's Eve, for instance, CBC Radio in St. John's was called upon to beam "The Image" across Canada. What happened wasn't at all pretty.

They tried to keep a foot on every possible base. There was an old-time, traditional, genuine, professional-Newfie "kitchen party" ashore and then more of similar was to be done aboard an offshore oil rig ... but the latter was cancelled when an iceberg came along.

And then — and then! — the whole mishmash was interspersed by the satirical troupe of CODCO and pals making merry mock of old-time, traditional, genuine, professional Newfies. Surely, there's some risk of a cultural hernia here.

To further confuse the Un-Newfie Activities Committee in each of us, there was a yuletide production of maunderings about the "traditional Newfoundland Christmas" featuring our adopted cosmopolitan thespian, Maxim Mazumdar, he being one of the Bombay, rather than one of the Bonne Bay, Mazumdars.

We Newfies spend most of our waking hours cursing the place and each other up in heaps. This shows our basic good sense and sound attitude. Other rustic and isolated settlements like Charlottetown, Calgary and Vancouver have the same admirable outlook.

It's all jolly larks as long as it's kept to ourselves. But let a peep, good, bad or indifferent, be wafted abroad and local reaction is savage. The miserable offender gets miniature hangman's nooses and second-hand kitty litter in the mail and telephonic suggestions that he move to "Comminis Rusher or Comminis Chiner." Or Halifax.

Older civilizations such as are found in Nova Scotia, Moncton or Toronto have long since settled on the self-image they will display to the outside world and they stick to it. Hence, all Christendom thinks of Nova Scotia when — and only when — macramé, Peggy's Cove, inferior smoked salmon, Harold Horwood or the Graveyard of the Atlantic are mentioned. And when the little aboriginal in the farthest reaches of the Amazonian jungle bewails floods, tumults, famine and yaws, its mother tells it to button its ungrateful lip, it could be living in Moncton.

Toronto, to the world, is where all unbaptized Italians and Newfies go when they die laughing, where Gordon Sinclair's mother was frightened by a Haligonian and where Buffalo is not.

These places have got their act together. They present a unified and coherent front. That's why they're able to attract such inestimable assets as CBC headquarters, CN warehouses and a regional magazine which descends to covered bridges and yet another fish chowder recipe only when times are really tough.

We in Newfie have much to do in that regard and so little time in which to do it. I fear it is already too late. If so, then next New Year's Eve broadcast out of CBC-St. John's may feature a drama in which an aged Newfie who's won the Lotto remarks: "Arrr, I minds the time when me poor fadder, the maharaja, entered the gates of our new palace in Bonne Bay and sez to me, he sez, 'Arrr, if your poor mother was alive today to see this she wouldn't half be as happy as a lamb on a headstone.' No, poor hand."

PARANOIA, XENOPHOBIA AND FOG: NEWFOUNDLAND AS A SPY PARADISE

Just after Hallowe'en, appropriately, a pair of "Cissys" were in town. They asked selected local journalists out to lunch. Why didn't they ask me?

Since they did not, Canada's new Civilian Intelligence Service, the CSIS, is off to a poor start here. They should have first beaten a path straight for my door — like the CIA and MI5 before them. It is not for nothing that I am known in better spy circles as "Der Smalischer Dicke" as in "a little dicky bird told me."

Of course, my many "friends" in the KGB know me by other less complimentary names. But what all these spooks have in common is the knowledge that if anyone has a firm grasp of local clandestine affairs it is "G." All, it seems, except the CSIS.

To be fair, these two bellwethers of the CSIS (I won't reveal their true identities here) must have been new to the job. My informants tell me that one of them wore black kid gloves throughout luncheon and that the other, posing as a local, refused to check his 200-pound halibut at the restaurant door. Not good enough, CSIS.

Yes, I am a little miffed by this snub. Unless, by the end of this month, I am met outside "Mammy Gosses" hootch dispensary on Gower Street by a six-foot blonde wearing a yellow rose who can recite "Mrs. Pudgywudgy's got a square-cut punt. . ." in its entirety (and in a flawless Bonavista North accent) then I shall be forced to take steps.

Steps guaranteed to shove pacemakers into overdrive inside those dark, forbidding Kremlin walls when it is learned that "G," the Scourge of the Eastern Bloc, is thinking of turning his coat.

It is not only this personal oversight by the CSIS which has ruffled the feathers of "Der Smalischer Dicke." It goes deeper. That any place other than Newfoundland should have been considered as HQ for Canada's new nest of spymasters is a national disgrace.

Ottawa? Don't make me barf down my trench coat. Montreal? Toronto? Keep me away from my Walther PPK.

No, only Newfoundland has got what it takes to be the spy centre of Canada ... plenty of fog, loads of paranoia, an abundance of xenophobia and more dark suspicions than James Bond has had hot dinners. Just ask Brian Peckford ... if that is, indeed, his real name.

Here on the "Fortress Isle" we've been practicing intrigue and cultivating our suspicions for centuries. No keener sense of "us versus them" is known to medical science. If someone sneezes in a foreign accent in Corner Brook, curtains twitch in front windows all the way to St. John's.

You wouldn't get the scandalous enemy infiltration for which Canada is notorious if the CSIS set up shop here. That's because we get only three kinds of strangers:(1) those who are just passing through;(2) those who've been up to no good where they came from;(3) those who've come here to get up to no good.

Your KGB chappie wouldn't stand a snowball's chance. "Byes, iss it beink true zat pickled herring quotas here in glorious Newfie peoples' village of Bung Hole Tickle are down from '84?" would get the poor shmuck a filleting knife in the brisket. They'd take him for a UIC snooper.

Newfoundland is impossible to infiltrate because everyone here is related to someone who knows someone else's Great-aunt Gert's second husband's third cousin on his mother's side.

Our precious God-given paranoia is well-served by our political leaders. In his latter years of power, Mr. Smallwood raved about sinister forces who were snooping and spreading false witness about him. He had his office swept for bugs.

Of course, Joey's real problem was that he hadn't been to a Bingo game or a tavern in years; it wasn't espionage but public opinion that was undermining him.

In late years, Premier Peckford had an eight-foot chain-link fence thrown up around his residence and a 24-hour guard installed. Cruel tongues said this wasn't so much to keep someone out as it was to keep Mrs. Peckford in ... unsuccessfully, as it turned out.

But this strong streak of suspicion, this conviction that "they" are out to get "us," is what endears our leaders to us — which, in turn, proves that we have the makings of damn fine spymasters.

We have faith in our politicians, we trust them, we look up to them. Our proudest boast is that there was never the Mafia chieftain yet born of woman who can out-scoundrel a Newfoundland Cabinet Minister. So, unlike Nancy Reagan, we do not sleep with tiny little guns under our pillows.

Added to all this (CSIS take note) we already have "moles" in place all over the world. Well, to be more precise, only three so far in China — Tom, Dick, and Gerrard of the "Little Hearts Ease Hand Laundry," Peking, but this is early days. On the other hand, Mrs. Gorbachev's hairdresser was weaned on fish and brewis ... and it shows.

There are tens of thousands of "former" Newfoundlanders scattered about the globe, cocked and primed, ready to dish out the exploding cigars, poison-tipped umbrellas and gelignite whoopie cushions as soon as the secret code is flashed from a powerful transmitter located somewhere deep in the heart of the Annieopsqotch Mountains.

Here we have crushing proof that CSIS headquarters should be in Newfoundland and nowhere else. On the one hand, not even a Cape Bretoner can get in here without detection; on the other, we can go anywhere and blend in with the scenery ... as our man on station for the past 36 years in the Hindu Kush can well verify.

Spy-wise, Newfoundland is unexcelled because we get few if any immigrants. The handful that do apply are subjected to a

60-day psychiatric examination and, unless found to be slightly nuts, are immediately deported as potential enemy agents. Even then, they're still under suspicion if not discovered crawling on hands and knees towards the plane for St. Pete's Beach, Fla., in the middle of March.

So, as noted above, the CSIS had better have that six-foot blonde with the yellow rose in front of "Mammy Gosses" by the end of this month. "Der Smalischer Dicke" is ready to dicker. Otherwise ... ?

Otherwise I fear for the security of Canada. Surrounded as she is by enemies without and within, the formation of a proper Civilian Intelligence Service, i.e., a Newfie one, is of the utmost importance.

Otherwise, as Tonto said to the Lone Ranger when they were trapped and encircled by 12,426 howling, blood-thirsty Sioux: "Speak for yourself, White Man."

A DISCREET INQUIRY INTO MORALS AT BUNG HOLE TICKLE

It's my custom to place a finger on the pulse of rural New-foundland from time to time. I drive out from the suave, swinging, sophisticated capital of St. John's and rusticate. No place serves my purpose better than the historic yet forward-looking little town of Bung Hole Tickle.

My last such socio-economic foray was in late April. As I motored westward through the streets of the city there were signs of spring on every hand. The six-foot snow drifts were melting with all the speed of the Waterton Lakes Glacier.

Perky little dead cats, defunct seagulls, discarded chicken boxes and abandoned sherry bottles peeked through slush here and there, harbingers of a greater lushness soon to come.

At intervals, the sidewalks were spangled with gay drifts of doggie-doo, dormant under winter's mantle since mid-December. My heart soared. It's either that or stick your head in a gas oven.

Out in the country it was colder, cleaner. Crows, ravens and gulls squabbled over the carcasses of Pintos, Mustangs and Ponies. Most of these had perished in terrible blizzards on the long trek south to St. Pete's Beach, Fla.

Midway along the route I halted my motor and stepped out to savour spring's onrush. The air was clear, crisp, invigorating. My fingers froze to my zipper.

Sounds of awakening nature were everywhere. From the myriad ponds and lakes came soft yet unmistakable "clunk-clunk-clunk" noises. Demented trout banging their heads against the ice.

Finally, Bung Hole Tickle was achieved. I stopped on a small promontory overlooking the town and gazed at the cozy habitation spread below me. Just then, from somewhere to my left came a strangled cry of anguish and despair:

"Be the lard liftin' jumped-up, sawed-off, reevin', dyin', merciful, almighty, sanctified Jeeee-rusalem ... " and more to that effect. I recognized it immediately as the voice of one of the town's revered elders, Uncle 'Posh Twaddle.

Though well up in years Uncle 'Posh is still spry and hale. His proudest boast is that he can still read his Bible without the aid of glasses. He drinks straight from the bottle.

I made myself known. "Good day, sir, good day, good day," he replied. "I never should have sold me little pony, Charles, and bought a heap of rubbish like this."

He was struggling with a motor toboggan that had quit. "But surely, Uncle," said I, "that machine must be useful to you as you gather your firewood, tend your traplines or simply commune with nature."

"Naw," spat Uncle 'Posh. "I've had enough of that old nonsense to last me a lifetime. 'Tis only the younger crowd goes in for that stuff now. I got the 'lectric heat and a mica-wave oven."

"No, what I got this for is if you, say, gets her up to top speed and points her at a knob like that one over there ... my son, she takes off in the air like the devil to wing. Give your liver a nice shakin' up."

As I drove him down to town we passed what looked to be a bombed-out suburb. Smoke rose from the ground which was littered with a vast array of furniture ... chairs, tables, sofas, stoves, refrigerators. It was the town dump, he said.

"My sonny boy. Everytime the fishplant goes on overtime there is fellers that guts their living rooms or kitchens completely and takes out all new stuff on the payments. Easy come, easy go."

Judging by the assortment of lightly used goods on the dump, frugality seemed to have fled Bung Hole Tickle for some place like Palm Beach. There was also an amazing variety of motor vehicles in front of many doors. Uncle 'Posh explained.

"No snow last year. No play for the snowmobiles. So the boys made sure they had a good supply of what they call bog-buggies put aside last fall in case. And some four-wheel drives for in between. Can't corner 'em."

I was amazed. The contrast between rampant consumption here and what we hear of poverty, unemployment and despair from the vantage point of St. John's was startling. I asked the old gentleman for his theory.

"Mightn't be every place like this," he said. "But we got the fish and youse in St. John's got the talk. Talk, talk, talk about gas and oil. Ha, talk yourselves a cheque and see what bank'll cash it."

I suppose I followed him. Maybe not. To change the subject, I asked him how he was doing since Mrs. Twaddle had crossed over.

"Oh, pretty good, my son," he said. "Pretty good. I been livin' in sin for the past year and a half with Aunt Mollie Pritchit. Me youngsters kicked up the big stink about it, threatened to have the clergy on us ... poor foolish young mortals."

Before I could ask the question he added: "Pensions, old man, pensions. If we gets hitched in the church they'll cut back our pensions. The good Lord wouldn't want to see good Christian people like we hove off on the welfare."

Merciful heaven! I thought. The little world of Bung Hole Tickle turned upside down. I enquired further about morality.

"Drugs? My dear man, something scandalous. Only last fall the Mounties broke in on a bunch in a summer shack just down the road. Never found nothin' ... but you know what they done? There was a Newfoundland dog there and the Mounties sent him all the way to Halifax to get X-rayed."

"Scandalous altogether. Is there no X-rays closer than Halifax? Cheese, Halifax gets it all."

Had this once-tranquil little town changed into a slough of vice, iniquity and greed? Perhaps even to the extent of voting Liberal? All the signs pointed out that way.

"The spring election, Uncle 'Posh," I said. "Was there any great swing away from Peckford?"

"Other way around, sir," he said. "We was nearly all for 'im. Figured if we gave him another couple years' rope he'd have enough to hang himself from the moon."

I sighed and shook my head sadly. All the rustic Newfoundland virtues consigned to the Bung Hole Tickle town dump and a mad dash, now, for filthy lucre and la dolce vita. Uncle interpreted my disapproval.

"These days," he said, "envy and $1.50 will get you a mug of tea."

THE TRUTH ABOUT RAM-CATS AND OTHER CREATURES FROM BEYOND

My household is ill-equipped and I dare say yours is too, for the lack of a hag board.

Should the Old Hag come a-calling, I'd have no defence except to say my name backward. The Lord's Prayer backward is also said to be efficacious. But nothing beats the board.

It's just a piece of board the size of your chest studded with sharp nails. You strap it to your body and go to sleep on your back. Then when the gruesome night visitor comes to sit on your chest and press the breath out of you she's in for a surprise.

Perfect slumber guaranteed — even though your more usual bed partner may end up looking like a colander.

Newfoundland has its fair share of ghosts, ghouls and other assorted characters from beyond although the spread of electricity and street lights seems to have cut seriously into the population.

Being "fairy led" can be an awkward problem. You're walking through the woods and the little folk cast a spell over you. Then they make you walk for miles in any direction you want.

So you must always carry a piece of hard tack ship's biscuit in your pocket as a sort of bribe for the fairies. Failing that, you snatch off your jacket, quick as a bunny, and put in on hind part before.

The fairies once caught a neighbour of ours. He was cutting firewood with some companions and hours later he found himself with a large log on his back — 10 or 15 miles from where he'd been. When a pious, godfearing gentleman who'd never think of telling the slightest untruths delivered this as a matter of fact report there's not much you can do but sit there and listen, your jaw slightly slack.

In Newfoundland when the evening assembly in some kitchen or other gets going on tales of the supernatural the beginning is almost invariably, "Of course now I don't believe in that stuff myself. It's just old superstition. But there was a strange thing happened to me once and I haven't been able to figure it out to this day."

An uncle of mine was on the Grand Banks in a schooner. Suddenly he and some others saw the figure of a stranger on deck. Uncle walked boldly up to it. It turned with blazing eyes and vanished.

They found out later, of course, that a man had recently drowned on the exact spot.

That particular kind of ghost is called a "fetch." A fetch is the spirit of someone dead. A "token" on the other hand is the ghost of someone at a distance and at the moment they die — or is it the other way around? My handle on ghostology is not what it once was.

Women especially seem to see tokens of absent relatives at the moment they meet disaster and find out days, perhaps weeks later that the worst is true.

Ghostly burning ships are fairly thick upon the water, often with spectres of dead seamen clearly visible in the rigging.

Poltergeists no longer keep the clergy as busy as they once did. These, of course, are not seen but cause objects to fly about. They seem to pester, in particular, girls in their mid-teens.

One of this variety of spook on Merasheen Island, Placentia Bay, had the double-whammy put on it by the priest three times before it skedaddled. At one point it looked like a job for the bishop.

Strange black dogs are not to be trifled with under any circumstances. It might be the devil in disguise. A test is to hold out your arm with just the little and index fingers sticking up and if it is the wicked gentleman his true features will appear.

Pirates or "Frenchmen" are sometimes seen sitting on the beach checking their accounts and taking inventory of their loot. There were always rumours of "Frenchman's gold" at my ancestral seat near Come By Chance. It's now thought to be relics of a Basque whaling station from the 1500s.

But once near this same spot a sailor's boot was found on the beach. Although it was tossed back in the ocean or buried in the earth some distance away it always moved itself back to the same spot. Trust me. Mother speaks only gospel.

"Strangers" are no longer as common as they were. These blokes look fairly normal, some of them quite well dressed. But if you do hail them in passing on a dark road they seem not to hear and look neither right nor left. Or they leave no footprints in the snow. Horses balk seriously at passing them.

Far as I know, we've never had truck nor trade with werewolves or vampires. But there's an appalling creature in animal form called a "ram-cat." It's 10 times the size of an ordinary moggie and so ferocious in appearance that it puts grown men off their feed for a week.

More benign phenomena were the speaking farm animals. Once a year on Old Christmas Day (Jan.6) they were granted the power of speech at midnight. This true believer never quite had the guts to eavesdrop outside a dark barn at that hour.

Not all the spooks out our way were what they seemed. One of them was an uncle of mine, a notorious prankster. His gimmick was to gallop past some wayfarer on a dark night and gather the sheet in a ball in front of him, thus "disappearing." More than one nervous nellie had to be brought around with massive applications of smelling salts.

Perhaps it isn't fair to call them that. Nearly everyone once believed in ghosts to one extent or the other. Most had an experience with one and it was hard to be a non-believer when some pillar of the community stated his vision in plain terms.

Me? Well, of course I don't believe in that old stuff but ... Once, as a lad, I was walking in the woods with my dog. I carried a telescope which I prized and somehow lost it.

For an hour I made a frantic search. Finally, I said to the dog, "Bounce. Spy glass." He made a direct beeline to where I had dropped it.

At that instant something literally lifted me about a mile above the earth so that I was looking down on a large chunk of Creation with the most powerful feelings of calm and joy ... I could see boats on the ocean maybe 50 miles distant.

Gospel truth. Any cracks about the state of my top storey and I'll sic my resident ram-cat on you.

WHAT DOES IT TAKE TO CAST DOWN A NEWFOUNDLANDER?

There may be joy in the tents of the righteous when they learn that this month's column was shot to hell because its blasphemous, stiff-necked and uncircumcised author couldn't locate a certain verse in the Bible.

"It is hard for thee to kick against the pricks," is the text in question.

I know it's there. I used it a few years ago in a piece for CBC Radio. They didn't believe it and wouldn't use the article until I was able to quote chapter and verse.

This time, sure that *Atlantic Insight* would demand similar proof, I tore back and forth through scriptures like a white shark in a feeding frenzy. It eluded me. The editor's last trump had sounded for the May deadline and I had to give it up.

The context of the quotation is a warning to sandal-shod citizens that they can no more kick a thorn bush with impunity than they can rebel against the word of God.

My plan for the column was this: Given that this past winter Newfoundlanders had received three nasty little bunny punches in a row ... (1) The Supreme Court gave Hibernia to poor little Ontario; (2) Quebec is permitted to suck dry Churchill Falls at a tremendously bloated profit and (3) Greenpeace drove us slack-jawed and bloody-handed barbarians from the seal hunt. Yet, for all these bad tidings, Newfoundlanders seemed just as happy-go-lucky as ever. There was no great despair. What in the world would it take, I wondered, to cast us down?

A Canada-U.S.S.R. accord giving Russian subs the right to use Newfoundland fishing dories for target practice? The new birth control method, tight underdrawers for men, entrenched in the Constitution for those east of North Sydney? Only oranges with mouldy spots on them to be allowed across the Cabot Strait?

All these and many more atrocities from the hand of man I considered, but saw that no such things would make us less high-stomached and that we would continue merry, yea, even like unto the jolly lambs which skippeth apace in springtime.

Nor princes nor principalities may lay us low, thought I, but what would be our estate if the face of a Higher Power were turned against us? Unlike Joey Smallwood or the late Wacky Bennett, I don't have a direct line to God, so I could only anticipate the actions of the frail instruments of His wrath. The Rev. Barry Lee Phartley, for instance, with his weekly message on 364 television and 192 radio stations. Suppose that the Rev. Barry Lee, having shot all the gays, expelled all the Jews and Democrats and having consigned Mother Teresa of Calcutta to hell's flames got fog-bound for his sins at Gander International for 18 hours and there discovered a whole island chock-a-block with godless, recalcitrant prick-kickers.

"The fingers of their little children, friends," the Rev. Phartley, rotund and sweating in his vanilla-linen suit, would roar into the cameras, "shall be held against EEEE-lekricly-driven emery wheels forevah!"

"And likewise," Barry Lee would continue in a purr, "the tiny little toes of the wretched seed of them Commie-lovin' idolators in Newfoundland shall be ground away to bloody nubs against the carborundum and, lo, there shall be no more OOOO-nanism and no more shall their little feet stray from the paths of righteousness. Hallelujah!"

Of course, you have grasped my difficulty right away. The Rev. would never have preached against Newfoundlanders' deadly sin of kicking against the wossanames without reference to the chapter and verse. That was a pity, because without Phartley I could hardly move along, in the interests of fair and balanced reporting, to the Holy See. There we might have found the Holy Father over his breakfast of Polish sausage and the daily report from around the globe: The Bank of Rome again, the

Freemasons, the Mosquito Indians, Imelda Marcos, Bulgarians, the Devil in Miss Jones, Julius Schmidt and the Rev. Barry Lee Phartley.

"Your Canadian tour prep sheets, Holiness," the Nuncio might have said. "This morning, Terra Nova, to put it in the Latin. Reports are terse and, ahem, Jesuitical. A fractious and aggressive race ... it says here. When they're not abusing someone else they're hard at it abusing themselves. Prick-kicking is also rumoured."

"Anathema!" sprang to His Holiness' lips. But, then, that same great spirit of charity which had brought Il Papa to the very jail cell of the Turk who had put a bullet through the Papal tripes gave His Holiness pause. He told his secretary to scratch that.

Self-abuse could not, however, be dismissed lightly. Heavy penance was indicated. He dictated a change in September's agenda.

"At Torbay, at St. John's, at Flatrock and even, due to fog, a detour through Mount Pearl, the faithful are commanded to turn out in droves but are directed, on pain of excommunication, not to look upon the Popemobile or the papal person."

"Scratch that, too," sighed His Holiness. "Our children in Terra Nova are in a decent Christian latitude, and there are excellent miners among them. A certain amount of self-abuse is admissible but wossaname-kicking is definitely out."

The Archbishop of Canterbury would not have seen it much differently. But Runcie, having the advantage of being an Englishman, could have told the Holy See a thing or two about keeping the heathen, white, black, yellow, brown and pink, in line. What empire had the Poles ever had, after all?

"No Royal visits for the next five years," directed his Lordship. "St. Paul tells us that wossaname-kicking must be looked at askance wherever it rears its ugly head. If, in 400 years, they haven't learned to eat with the fork held in the left hand, then not so much as a touchdown at Gander International by so much as the Princess Margaret Rose!"

About the only bright spot for Newfoundlanders, now that the face of God was turned away from them would have been the Ayatollah Khomeini. In the medieval backwaters of Islam, prick-kicking was not held in any special esteem nor yet was it abhorred. Practitioners were simply given a special armband and put in the forefront of the holy war against everyone else.

Young Alfie Peckford would have hesitated for a moment when the proposition from Ayatollah arrived that New-foundlanders be made honourary Shi'ites, but then would have gone ahead and shipped off five boatloads Cash On Delivery.

Would Newfoundlanders be any less cheerful and sure of themselves with the hand of BOTH God and man turned against them? Alas, we may never know.

But caution: Smiting us with boils from head to foot by allowing nothing but rotten oranges to cross the Cabot Strait will get you nowhere. It's been done and tossed off as child's play. To put our motto into the Latin, Terra Novum Bootae Arsum Toujours.

TUNING IN TO A SLICE OF LIFE

On mornings when your head feels like a sun-split turnip, your eyeballs are sandpapered and your tongue would be of interest to the Hudson's Bay Company, there's no better counter-irritant than the radio open-line shows.

If these things have any virtues, this is their chief one. Instead of drop-kicking the cat through the kitchen window or tossing live geraniums into the furnace, you can pour out all your pique toward the radio. Open-line shows are the Preparation H of broadcasting.

We have several in this neck of the woods. It's nice to have a choice, because if you tire of ignorance you can cut across the dial to prejudice and then back again. Of course, the callers to both are the same two-dozen Valium and/or gin addicts leavened by the occasional fresh UFO.

In charge of the microphone and buttons is the crypto-Nazi who calls himself the "host" or the "moderator" and whose main task is to remind callers either that they're full of garbage or that they've forgotten to turn down their radios. Most moderators are refreshingly right wing. Ours are known affectionately as Adolph and Benito.

Bring Back the Lash is their favourite topic on slow mornings. To these birds, the lash is modern molly-coddling, and a return to the rack, the stake and the iron maiden is the only thing that warms their cockles. For gleeful savagery, they are surpassed only by some who have missed their true vocation as prison wardresses in Paraguay.

To be fair, though, the moderators constantly struggle to lift the tone. Their opening pep talk now and then promises a subject that's of "tremendous importance to every living soul on this globe today, possibly the most important situation that has ever faced the human race." First caller: "I bought a chesterfield suite up to Steinberg's six months ago and, you know what, the legs is already fallin' off 'en!"

An odd thing about open-line shows is that they seem to be immune to the normal laws of libel and slander, especially now when other editors and producers show an unhealthy fear of such nonsense.

One morning, I was titillated to hear: " ... and do you know there's a 'omosixual ring of teenage boys bein' operated by a certain person in this man's town today? It might h'interest some of your listeners to know the name of a certain assistant manager of a certain branch of the Bank of Nova ... " Click.

Actually, it was another bank that was as good as named. But there aren't that many banks in this man's town. The damage done, mine host merely remarked: "My gawd, they're coming out of the woodwork again this morning."

That's what Adolph said on another occasion when Benito was off the air due to his being in court as a defendant, as everyone knew.

"You got the airwaves all to yourself this morning, Adolph, old son," said a caller.

"What's that? What's your point? We must have a bad line here, speak up, speak up."

"I said, you got the airwaves all to yourself," shouted the caller. "The other feller been dragged up in court in front of the judge."

"You're still not making any sense here. Get to the point. Speak up, speak up."

Roared the goaded caller: "The feller with the other show, your competition on the other station, he been dragged into court for tryin' to skip around the laws of this land once too often!" Click. "My gawd, they're coming out of the ... ." et cetera.

Moderators change now and then, but the callers never seem to. A fixture since the last Ice Age was a former nun who had kicked the habit long since due to physical, spiritual and mental difficulties. She was thus the right stuff for open-line programs.

Her forte was reading uplifting verse of her own composition. As the years, yea, the decades passed, she drifted steadily toward the dangerous shoals of plagiarism. On the eve of a royal visit, she burned the midnight oil on an ode to the occasion that began: "Susanne takes me down to her place by the river ... "

As time goes by, you may check in occasionally and trace the intimate ups and downs of the regulars — their changes of medication, their nervous disorders, their gradual decline into senility. You can do the same with columnists. But the difference is, these poor old biddies are not paid a cent and are simply baited for the fun and profit of others.

Open-line hosts are soon drawn into the "community service" competitions that go on among radio stations. Our two networks have become so strident in their profession of caring and sharing that you'd swear one outfit was run by Albert Schweitzer and the other by Florence Nightingale. Truth to tell, a principal in one case is so parsimonious he has refused to pay upkeep on his wife's grave from the day she was planted.

Competition in the self-promotional charity gambit gets so fierce at times that the pleas on behalf of the needy soar. Between battles, the call may be for nothing more than a second-hand baby crib; at fever pitch, complete houses are solicited. A year or so ago, residents of the nearby French islands of St. Pierre overheard and were so aghast at the apparent destitution in Newfoundland that they started shipping over CARE packages.

The real value of open-line radio programs may be as a counterbalance to that view of society held by the establishment.

Take the Pope's visit. Leaders of church, state and commerce are gushing ecumenical sanctimony at both ends about the lack of bigotry, dissension and religious friction here in the Happy Province. Had there been an overnight miracle?

If you pay attention to open-line programs you're not so sure. For months, now, there's been the odd squawk from this supposed nest of singing birds. An example:

Mrs. Phone Forum (the regulars soon acquire noms des bouches) rang in the other day to say, certainly, there should be a public holiday for the visit ... not to have one would be blasphemous. A few years back, she said, she was a martyr to a bad head and she went to Monsignor Lawlor for laying on of hands and hasn't had a twinge since. If she could only touch the Holy Father, she said, she would want to die, being then perfect in body, mind and soul, at that very instant and that was God's truth.

"She makes my blood boil," immediately riposted The Old Man of the Sea. "If the commander of the Salvation Army put his hands on her, would that have the same effect? Or the feller in charge of the Church of Englanders, or so on?

"The Pope," said the OM of the S, "I got nothing at all against that feller. But you go to work and you put a .22 bullet into 'en and he'll drop right in his tracks, just the same as any other man."

I don't know if the Old Man has since been having chats with the Mounties or if Mrs. Forum's migraines returned, but I do know it's only on the often-despised open-lines that you get this close, without leaving the house, to social reality.

DEALING WITH DIALECTS

U p the Shi'ites!" roared the fellow getting into a St. John's airport taxi ahead of us. Our own driver sneezed violently and muttered, "Mary and Joseph, I'm Persian, Persian, Persian."

The person sharing the cab with me looked a little wild-eyed. I wondered if Air Canada had given him too much gin and too little oxygen. But since he'd got on at Moncton I figured it was simply jet lag and culture shock.

"It's the Middle Eastern influence," I explained to him kindly. "Hibernia draws people from all over."

He gave me a bilious glance and whipped a copy of the Newfoundland phrase book out of his valise.

"Don't try to get fresh with me, ducks," he snapped. "The first fellow was ordering his taxi driver to take him 'up to Shea Heights', a community that's part of St. John's and lies athwart the Southside Hills. Formerly it was known as the Brow or the Blackhead Road and was renamed for the late Father Shea who taught some of the residents not to hold their chain saws by the wrong end and did many other good works too numerous to count on the fingers of both hands!

"There," he said, triumphantly. "You must not attempt to josh an accomplished linguist who hails from Sackville in the picture province of New Brunswick."

"And what does Sackville lie athwart?" I riposted. "No, let me guess. Sackville, a town of 7,683 souls lying athwart the southeast flanks of lofty Mount Allison and named after the first settlers, a large family of Sacks, whose patriarch was Gunther and who, with Alexander Graham Bell, invented the Sacksaphone.

"No, no, I tell a lie. That's another Sackville. The New Brunswick Sackville takes its name from the famous retailing family of Fifth Avenue in New York.

"In the early part of this century, if memory serves me, the Sacks of Fifth Avenue built a huge summer home on the slopes of another Mount Allison which they named 'Munchiewunchie', an old Indian term meaning 'place where potato chips come in plain, salt or vinegar'.

"Mr. Charlie Sack, in particular, was noted for his philanthropy towards the natives. The history books record that about 1910 there was great distress among the scattered inhabitants of New Brunswick. They had lots of potatoes but nothing to put them in ... or nothing in which to put them as your linguistic purist would have it.

"So Old Mister Charlie, as he is affectionately known to this very day around Sackville, mentioned this to his great and good crony, Alexander Graham Bell, and between them they invented the desperately needed container for potatoes.

"Despite strenuous objections from the then-nonpowerful Irving interests", I continued, "they named their invention a Sack, a word which like Coke or Aspirin is still under patent but is used generically by the semi-literate among us.

"In fact, to this very day, the only employment in Sackville — apart from some minor gravel quarrying in the foothills of Mount Allison — is a huge burlap manufactory which at peak periods ... "

Had not our taxi driver again sneezed violently my fellow passenger would have screamed at me petulantly to shut up my bloody face.

"Cheese," said the driver, "I'm Persian, Persian, PERSIAN!"

"Ah, yes, when the old Shah fell," I explained generously, "some of the royal family of Iran fared but poorly, indeed. It's not every day you're going to get driven in from an airport by the third in line to the Peacock Throne.

"But you're still proud to be Persian aren't you, Prince Ahmed, old cock, and not one little bit ashamed to let all the accomplished linguists in Sackville know it, either."

"Perishing, not Persian!" said the Sackville linguist pounding me on the arm with his Newfoundland phrase book. "It says right here ...

"Quote. Persian, a corruption of perishing as in damn near dead with a nasty dose of this old grout that's on the go. Usually associated with colds or flu. When a Newfoundlander tells you he's 'Persian' he doesn't mean he's been hopping on and off the Peacock Throne all day.

"It continues. The worse the speaker feels, the more vehemently he will insist that he's Persian as in, 'Cheese, I'm Persian, Persian, PERSIAN!' It is then risky to either offer him a piece of cheddar or remark that while you yourself have always lived in Sackville you once had a cousin who did missionary work in Persia.

"Thus, 'Persian,'" I said, and "Achoo" said the driver. My fellow passenger was sunk deep in thought, much deeper and he'd have a serious case of the bends.

"Tell us a little more about Sackville," I said in an effort to keep the conversation alive. "Do you still have those world renowned races every year?"

A low growl was building up in his throat but I persisted in my efforts to be friendly and charming and so add a little to that vast ocean of Atlantic fraternity and solidarity as is my wont.

"I passed through Sackville, once," I said, "and the strange thing is, that for love nor money I couldn't find a sample of your most famous product to bring back as a souvenir, although I have seen lovely designer models at Sacks, Fifth Avenue which is odd because ... " and the growl got loud indeed.

"Cheese," said the driver, "would you fellows keep it down to a dull roar back there. I got one of these real savage Lunenburg headaches on me hands."

I think our visitor giggled. Or he might have been whimpering. It was hard to tell.

"Where did you say you was goin' again sport?" the driver asked me and I gave him the address of my current domicile.

"Ah, yes", he said. "Right behind the Lunatic."

"Oh, no you don't," said our visitor wildly. "That lunatic gets out behind me. I had this taxi first and ... "

"Page 57," I said. "Newfoundland phrase book. Right behind the Lunatic ... a phrase used by some taxi drivers to confirm an

address in one of the nicer areas of St. John's near beautiful
Bowring Park.

"A nearby hospital was once referred to as the Lunatic
Asylum. 'Right behind the Lunatic' is an earlier form of 'Right
behind the Mental' or the more modern, 'Up back of the Waterford,' you see, and should never be confused with ... "

A good chance we were on a stoplight. Our visitor leapt from
the cab and took off like a streak of lightning down Temperance
Street toward the Harbour.

He spoke a broad Sackville dialect, of course, but what he
was shouting sounded mighty like, "Up the Shi'ites! Up the
Shi'ites!"

OF OIL AND RICHES

THE NEW BLUE-EYED ARABS ARE NEWFOUNDLANDERS

Have you heard about the non-Newfoundlander who came to grips with the energy crisis by designing himself a unique solar-heated house? He plans to build it directly on top of the North Pole so the windows on all four sides face south. Here in Newfoundland, now that we've struck gas and oil, we can afford to snicker at what mainlanders regard as a serious subject. Even now, as the evenings draw in, we remain nonchalant about the "crisis" yet not, I hope, smug.

That old endearing humility is still there. No fleets of Cadillacs, no offers from us to purchase Windsor Castle. Puzzled mainlanders wonder why we don't sheik it up a bit. For instance, the other day as I was seated in a Water Street public house idly leafing through my Koran, a woebegone commercial traveler from across the Gulf slumped into the seat beside me. He dealt, as it turned out, in the export of falcons from British Columbia. As soon as he heard about our good fortune he told Prince Faisal to hold the phone and hiked himself along to St. John's. But in a single morning he'd been chucked out of three cabinet ministers' offices and his brace of Mussulman budgies pitched after him.

"What sort of freshly oil-crazed people are you?" he moaned. "In Muscat and Oman there's not a door that isn't open to me."

"I'll try to explain, old man," I said, as I ordered up a double for the poor beggar. "The gist of it is that being power-rich is old hat to us. We've been there before."

The first time you strike the energy jackpot (I continued), you're apt to be gauche. Take Albertans. Unlike us, they've had no prior experience in holding the upper energy hand and it's inflated their Stetsons. Albertans, supposing the last light on Bay Street flickered out, wouldn't ship those poor Ontarians down so much as a box-car load of buffalo chips. That's not us. Even the first time we struck the mother lode we were generous to a fault. Chummy's ears perked up, and to underline my point I ordered a couple of pickled pig's knucks for his birds.

Churchill Falls ring a bell? I said. There you go then. Did you know that at one time we had our hooks on enough electricity to ... well, if it was all wired into New Brunswick they'd be digging baked potatoes. We were tempted, it is true. We were beguiled by the prospect of three squares a day and less than 20% unemployment. But when it came right down to a choice between that sort of godless hedonism and being scared to touch a hydro pole on a wet day we chose the sterner path.

That old seductress, Wealth, should never have expected to get a purchase on a plain and simple folk like Newfoundlanders. There's more to life, isn't there, old man, than being able to ship Prince Philip off a fresh load of polo ponies every time the last batch gets sweaty or to engage Roloff Beny to take snaps of your porphyry pissoir? Of course, it wasn't all that simple. Once the word about Churchill Falls got out we couldn't leave it to simply tinkle over the rocks. By and by, the place would have been crawling with Rothschilds and du Ponts trying to force their filthy lucre on us.

Besides which, Premier Smallwood's birthday was coming up soon and so we decided to kill two birds with one stone ... as per your two bloody Persian parrots there, old man, if you don't unlatch them from my shins. We pressed ahead and dammed the dratted Churchill. This removed those pesky developers from our backs and it also created a reservoir which we named — in plenty of time for his birthday — the Smallwood Lake.

Our Ayatollah Cockamamie was then able to rise in the House of Assembly and report that Smallwood Lake was "seven times larger, Mr. Speaker, than the Sea of Galilee!" It was well worth it. We can now smile indulgently and hold up our heads when we hear Albertans boast that High River has five times more indoor plumbing than the Little Town of Bethlehem. That's the sort of feeling that can never be measured in megawatts or computed in white she-camels.

We were nearly out of the woods. One small detail remained. Here was Churchill Falls harnessed to create Smallwood Lake and the whole concern heaving off vast whacks of juice but nowhere to put it. We certainly didn't want the stuff ourselves. There's precious little advantage in having your toast pop twice as high. No problem at all to one who could now look down his nose at, if not perambulate on, the Sea of Galilee. Pass the juice over to Quebec! That way we got to keep the new lake without being encumbered by all those silly sparks.

In the true spirit of Confederation, Quebec took Churchill Falls hydro off our hands. Some mainlanders, with their peculiar mercenary ethos, claim the gift should have taken the sting out of the Plains of Abraham. But Smallwood continues to lecture the rest of us on the necessity of being kinder to Quebec. So there you are, old son (I said to the falcon retailer), there's Newfoundlanders for you when it comes to panache and the beau geste when faced with the threat of prosperity.

He said it did him worlds of good to have the Newfoundland psyche explained to him and thus to know that he really hadn't become the Willie Loman of the falcon-hawking world. There was actually a tear in his eye as he told me he'd never met a people with such a noble determination to remain poverty-stricken yet traditionally hospitable.

This touched me so much I offered him a half-dozen clapped-out hamsters I had kicking around the house as a special treat for his birdies. Hamsters don't last long when they're on the exercise wheel half the night keeping your bedside light aglimmer.

GOLD! NFLD. RICH! MINK-LINED YARMULKAS FOR ALL. WHO CARES?

"Gold!" rang out the thrilling cry in early summer. "Gold! Gold in abundance! It's a major strike!"

This is probably true. In the mountains of the southwest corner of Newfoundland is said to be the largest Canadian gold discovery in years. Yet public reaction was curious.

There was no frantic scramble for the hills. Sourdoughs were no-shows. Visitors remarked on the tremendous number of dynamite blasts that weren't and were amazed at the great crowds of eager young men not flocking to the goldfields.

"Naw, think I'll wait," was a common response among maggoty-headed young layabouts on Water Street. "Think I'll wait until they stumbles across diamonds on the South Side Hills."

In summer, Newfoundlanders don't believe. Not the weather forecast nor the Second Coming nor that the head bone is connected to the neck bone. Even politicians don't believe if the temperature gets much past 70 degrees Fahrenheit.

An Israeli outfit popped a plan to revive the moribund oil refinery at Come By Chance and set up a petro-chemical complex that would create 11,000 jobs.

The Peckford gang moaned with boredom and tried to look the other way. They acted as if 11,000 jobs would be the deuce of an encumbrance to Newfoundland. Had it been January instead of June the Ruhr Valley would not have stood up to Come By Chance in the local political rhetoric.

To understand our heedless attitude in summer you have to remember the story of Rover of the Goulds.

The Goulds is a farming area near St. John's and Rover was a horse. His owner advertised Rover for sale. When a prospective buyer came along Rover was far down the back field.

His owner called him and he started toward them at a brisk gallop. He ran head first into a tree and knocked himself out. It was the one and only tree in the entire acreage.

"That horse is blind," said the would-be buyer.

"Naa, boy," said Rover's owner. "That's just his carefree manner. That's only his way. Rover just don't give a bleep!"

Same with people here in summer. They don't give a fig for gold bonanzas, petro-chemical complexes or a policeman running down the street.

Of course, there's a second theory which discounts temperature altogether. It's that Newfoundlanders have developed a Pavlovian response when threatened with still more immense riches. When the burden of yet more incredible wealth is forecast we take fright and dive under the bed.

Small wonder. The more chaw there's been about offshore gas and oil the higher the unemployment figures went. A major gold strike (or at least the speculation thereof) can only mean pestilence, corruption, poverty and showers of toads.

If memory serves, Newfoundland has the lowest bond market credit rating in Canada. Possible gold in abundance doesn't seem to amuse Wall Street. Present potato crops in P.E.I. interest them more.

As to the local laity, it is reduced to believing nothing it hears and only half it sees.

A sort of battle fatigue is what it is. The strict medical term for it is "Come By Chance complex." As in "Come By Chance is gone, by God."

Ah, fair Come By Chance, my natal seat. The legend is that sometime in the mid-1700s, two jolly sailors were marooned in Placentia Bay for interfering with the captain's wife ... constant fog being especially good for the gonads.

One was put off on an islet with some bread and the other on a rock nearby with some cheese. These islands are still called

"The Bread and Cheese." Somehow they got together, made a raft and drifted ashore at ... Come By Chance!

A likely story, perhaps. In modern times two other scallywags, Smallwood and Shaheen, battened on Come By Chance. Half a billion dollars later the hallucinogenic remains of a moribund oil refinery stick up out of the C. by C. vapours.

More to come. When the refinery semi-ruins were put up on auction, two of those in the running were Mr. Shaheen and Israel. John Crosbie is said to support Tel Aviv while former premier Frank Moores champions Shaheen.

Those who don't know or remember how long, how viciously and how recently Frank Moores sought to kick Shaheen out of Come By Chance can't hope to understand what this latest slew-about does to the Newfoundland head.

You tend to strum the lower lip with a forefinger and gaze off at a non-existent horizon.

Gold in them thar hills? Yeah, sure. Diamonds in the South Side Hills? You bet. Toothbrush handles tumbling out of the vast factories at Come By Chance? Yes, I dare say.

In my own poor case it is, naturally enough, the situation at Come By Chance which most affects my reason. I have seen what was then the biggest bankruptcy in Canadian history transpire ... and seen it from the window where my crib used to be in a house in a village then of 186 people.

Now, Petro-chemicals and the Israelis. May the peace of God which passeth all understanding give us a hand here, will ya? Exocet missiles stacked up devil deep where the old sheep shed used to be?

The Moussad secret service (Come By Chance branch) headquartered in the old school house? ... although it would then be a damn sight more tranquil and less savage an ambience than when the building was a schoolhouse.

I dunno. The only bright spot is that it would solve part of my Christmas shopping list — Mother and Father to get one yarmulka apiece, gift wrapped. And mink-lined, or course.

An odd summer, this. Any strands of confidence or belief between government and people are snapping like rusty guy wires.

The gang at Confederation Building seems as punch-drunk as everyone else.

Tourists marvel at the traffic jams and bulging pubs on Water Street at 3 a.m. on Saturday mornings. Nothing like it, some say, in the whole of Canada except possibly Montreal. "Yuppie-ism" has struck with a vengeance and quarter-million dollar houses are springing out of the scrubby spruce.

Somebody has got money but it sure isn't the vast majority. Armed robberies have soared but money may not be the object there. A measly few bucks for an almost guaranteed couple of years in the clink makes little sense.

More likely boredom or an urge to lash out any which way or a knee-jerk reaction to the general sense of limbo and in-stability. I wasn't there but I saw the movie. The last days of the Weimar Republic must have been a tiny bit like this.

Sorry for any incoherence but I had a razzer hart night out at ze "Blue Angel" last night.

AT HOME WITH BUNG HOLE TICKLE'S SMART SET

G iven the times, it's curious that magazines for the filthy rich seem to be on the increase. Some of the old ones continue to prosper, of course. I dare say *The New Yorker* carries ads yet for shoes at "690.00 the pair" ... with nothing so common as a dollar sign attached.

Architectural Digest continues to tell us how we, too, can approach the good taste of the Aga Khan who has lately redecorated his bedroom, a cozy nook roughly the size of St. Peter's Basilica.

In the U.K., *Country Life*, founded shortly after the death of King Canute and still sounding like it, continues to prosper:

"Correspondence. The Lord Camperdown writes. 'Sir, I wonder if any of your readers have had the experience of being struck in the left eye by a greater blue tit. I was about to chastise my elderly Labrador bitch, which had defecated into my trouser turnups, when the tit flew out of a copse and struck me full in the face. It suffered no apparent harm. This curious incident so astonished me that I immediately sent for an undergardener and beat him to within an inch of his life.'"

And *Country Life* real estate ads have kept up standards, too: "An important manor house of elegance and charm with six main reception rooms, 15 principal bedrooms, 25 secondary bedrooms, one bathroom, usual offices, outbuildings, cottages, paddocks, pheasants, peasants, with about three quarters of the Home Counties in all for sale freehold."

The style of the newer posh mags is not so much different. Either *Vanity Fair* or *Vogue* is having a revival, I believe, and the November issue of the U.S. *Town and Country* was given over entirely to "The Canadians." Which Canadians are THE Canadians? Only those who buy shoes at 690.00 the pair, so you're not in there and neither is your Auntie Gertrude.

Sherry Eaton is there, all slung about with rocks the size of pullet's eggs; Conrad Black is there surveying his half of Ontario; Mr. and Mrs. Schenley Schweppes are there in their lovely house designed by Arthur Erickson with their two lovely children, also designed by Arthur Erickson.

A hefty section of "The Canadians" issue is devoted to snaps, by Karsh, of the True North's foremost, that is to say, richest, broads. A thumbnail sketch of their busy lives and penetrating philosophies is appended and full credit given to those who bejewelled, beclothed, bepainted and even beseated them, e.g., "Gown, Holt Renfrew; Jewelry, Bulgari; Makeup, Diane von Furstenberg, styled by Anita Varone of La Coupe; Fur, Grosvenor Fur from Fur Galleria; Chair, Florian Papp."

Peter Newman (quelle surprise!) leads off the issue with a wallowing dotage on the high and the mighty, and Kildare Dobbs contributes bits on just about every subject except the state of Canadian proctology. Vancouver, Calgary, Toronto and Montreal take most of the editorial space, and the Maritimes get dick-all in a brown paper bag and Newfoundland even less.

What does the Happy Province rate out of the magazine's 360 pages? Cod tongues are transferred to New Brunswick — and it can bloody well have them, far as I'm concerned. There's a brief mention of Christopher Pratt and, strangely, a large snap of Joey Smallwood. "Joseph R. Smallwood: Clothes, Garments Without Seam Inc.; Jewelry, Knuckle Dusters Boutique; Makeup, Maurice of Brass Monkey; Hair, Chez Gaule; Accessories, Doyle of Panama and Liechtenstein."

But that's about it. We just don't have enough filthy rich here to cut ice with the nob mags. We do have an abundance of stinking poor, and maybe they can be persuaded to titillate their jaded readers with the occasional slum-crawl. This is already done in some of the ads. Here's a skeletal young thing in $90,000 worth of Russian Sables, daring a bunch of beer-belly boys leaning on their jackhammers to pelt her. Or another sour-looking anorexic swinging fathoms of black pearls under the nose of a tattered connoisseur of domestic sherry.

What they do in the ads they could also do in the articles. For instance, as a piquant divertissement (nob mags lapse into Frogese at the drop of a chapeau) to all those Eatons, Blacks, Bassetts and Southams, they might give us Gertie Twigmire.

"A striking beauty and active member of the colourful Twigmire bootlegging and sporting family, Gertie lives in Bung Hole Tickle where husband Phonse Twigmore is president and chief executive of Twigmore's Amusement Parlour. From one of Bung Hole Tickle's original aristocratic families (an entire wing at H.M. Gaol is named after them), Gertie splits her time between the Legion beverage room, the District Home for Wayward Girls and the maternity wards, as a participating rather than a contributing benefactress.

"Jewelry, Chique Plastique; Dress, Ee-Zee-Off Creations; Fur, Miss Meow; Makeup, Benjamin Moore; Chair, the kitchen.

Another aspect of this is that the deluxe magazines might do well to get a foot in on the bottom floor with such as La Twigmire. For the day will surely come, as young Alfie Peckford never tires of telling us, when St. John's will import its domestic help from Dallas, and Peter Newman will torch an orphanage to get to one of Gertie and Phonse's bunfights.

After all, what was Calgary until not so long ago? A fragrant little cow town where the men were men and the cows were running scared. You couldn't get a decent pig's knuck quiche in the whole of Montreal until that little town was lifted high on beaver pelts and Schenley's home-brew holy water.

Vancouver did not become the great orifice de debouchement it is today until a railway broke the natural constipation of the Prairies; nobody in his right mind, except Jamaicans, Newfoundlanders and southern Italians, would move to Toronto until Jamaicans, Newfoundlanders and southern Italians did.

So our turn will come sooner or later, although at this rate of progress, by the time it does, Gertie Twigmore will be the grand old bag of the filthy rich Twigmore clan, which will have recently purchased both *Town and Country* and Peter Newman.

A captain of commerce like Phonse Twigmore III is not going to take kindly to a continent, let alone a posh magazine, that cut his dear old granny away back in 1983.

"Be nice to people on your way up," goes the old saying, "because you'll need friends on the way down."

That may be so, but what Joey Smallwood ever did for the Hearst Corp., publishers of *Town and Country*, is beyond me. Perhaps some of our readers can advise. I must end our correspondence now, as it smells as though my elderly Labrador bitch has been up to her old tricks again.

Cheers. Guy, Compte de Come By Chance.

WHAT ATLANTIC CANADA NEEDS: AN ACROPOLIS UP IN THE HILLS

At this rate we'll go down to paupers' graves with the Great Dream of a united Atlantic Canada still up in slings.

Decades roll into history and we're still the scattered and impoverished tribes we always were: feuding, quarreling, fractious, each clinging petulantly to his tattered dignity, Halifax disparaging St. John's, Moncton scornful of North Sydney.

Where is the long-awaited "Atlantic Accord", the pooling of resources, the consolidated demographical clout, the great upsurge of brotherly accord founded on a common root and nurtured in shared latitudes?

Up Sissiboo Creek without a paddle, far as I can see.

This great drawing together of Atlantic peoples for their mutual entertainment and to screw a few extra sheckles out of Ottawa has got us nowhere.

Meanwhile, we continue to be mocked in our penurious disarray by the great, placid, milk-fed corn-stodged fact of Ontario, sleek and wallowing in surfeit yet agile enough to dart at and slurp any shreds of nourishment drifting our way. It's enough to give the Holy Ghost a haemorrhage.

Quite so ... and another eight-month winter staring us straight in the face on top of it. I at first contemplated a frantic telegram to Harry Flemming. But then I sprang for solace, as is my wont, to Scriptures:

"And the city lieth foursquare and the length is as large as the breadth ... and the building of the wall of it was of jasper and the city was pure gold like unto clear glass ... "

Joey Smallwood, when in his prime, used to think a lot like that particularly when it came to Churchill Falls or Come By Chance, I mused.

I suppose it was the chance conjunction of Smallwood and St. John the Divine which caused a mighty explosion in my higher consciousness like unto a great overdose of psychic epsom salts.

For there it was! We've been doing it all back foremost. City first ... and then, and only then, your conferences of Atlantic premiers, your Atlantic Provinces Economic Councils, your cultural exchanges of Atlantic Bingo Callers and the rest.

A new capital city for Atlantic Canada is what is wanted. Away with musty Fredericton, perish pretentious Halifax, avaunt thee poxy St. John's, begone garish Charlottetown. Nothing less than a New Jerusalem will do us now.

Brazil had done it with Brasilia; Australia did it with Canberra; Canada itself did it with Ottawa — and look what nests of singing birds they all are today.

The main thing about a new capital city is that it's got to be central. Another point in favour is that it be "builded upon an high mountain", if the Word of God is anything to go by. That cuts out Nova Scotia which has got few hills above knee height, and P.E.I. which is actually below sea level and New Brunswick which is lofty in spots but pressed too hard by "Them" to the south and "Les autres" to the westward.

"Cape Breton" might spring to the lips of an ignorant few. Why not Cape Breton as the new seat of brotherly Atlantic accord? Because that lot is too contrary to even get along with its sheep, as the rest of us know only too well.

So I submit, as the popular choice, the magnificent 2,600-foot Lewis Hills in Western Wossaname. A splendid prospect, a neutral location, agreeable to all concerned. And beautiful downtown Corner Brook just a few short miles away — with colour TV only $4.95 extra in all rooms.

To forestall certain civil war, some outfit from Stockholm or Yokohama will have to be hauled in to build this monument to Atlantic felicity. I see no problem with federal funds if ... if the first thing in place is a great hairy heliport the like of which has not been seen outside of Star Wars.

Because, you see, the civil servant has not yet been born of woman who doesn't fancy himself scuttling away in a semi-crouch from a helicopter with a couple of brace of whey-faced minions in tow.

If you guarantee an Ottawa bureaucrat a snap of himself on the front page of the Citizen skittering away from a helicopter he'll rip the bottom out of his goodie bag for you with his bare fingernails.

Colorado might be our best bet for an architect. You run across them in that region hanging out of the cacti and yarry for another round. For the price of a bottle they'll knock you up a spectacular born-again TV tabernacle — or a new Woolco-Atlantis and/or Jerusalem half-way up the Lewis Hills.

High notions we must have but, in this day of rising inflation and the 10-cent ciggy, a few corners will have to be cut. For instance, chrysoprasus. The tenth part of the Biblical new town (Revelation, 22:20) was built of such. In our poor case, angel stone will have to do.

Dignity, yes. Grandeur, certainly. But I'd say we could forego those items with "the shapes of locusts like unto horses prepared unto battle, on their heads as it were crowns of gold and faces as the faces of men ... " (Rev. 9:7) lurking behind the alabaster pillars. A few former cabinet ministers scattered about would do as well.

We're going to get the average Sarnia, Ont., tourist on his two weeks' annual visiting our new capital and we don't want stuff that might pitch the missus into hysterics and the youngsters into having a misfortune in their pants right there in the Great Hall of the Scotias.

Besides, you could load the joint to the gunwales with Scriptural chrysoprasus, sardonyx, chalcedony and high-grade colour-lok siding and some boorish little heifer-hugger from Alberta would still say, "pooh, not a pimple on the new Edmonton Mall."

Our new Acropolis should dazzle the lesser breeds but at the same time reflect our roots. Decor must be Versailles-ish yet earthy. Spuds, for instance, dangling from the rafters of Le Grand Salon des Irish Cobblers (formerly P.E.I. Place) in individual little macrame bags.

By now I expect you have the picture. A new Cultural focus and spiritual home for all Atlantic people. Atlantic unity, harmony, cooperation — the Great Desire of the Ages — finds a fitting abode at last.

Just as soon as we can swing a DREE grant the cornerstone should be laid. And who better to lay it than the dean of Atlantic premiers, Mr. Hatfield. Then, by satellite link, the symbolic embrace of unity by all four political leaders.

These grand ceremonies will be attended by thousands and should be open to anyone — anyone who holds a valid Newfoundland passport, available half-price on weekends from the kiosk behind the Pepsi machine at the CN ferry terminal, Port aux Basques.

A STORM OF WEATHER
BAFFLEGAB

The North wind doth blow
We shall have snow
What will the Robin do then
  Poor thing?

O r, to put it another way, winds are currently out of the north at 46 kilometres per hour, the temperature is minus six degrees Celsius resulting in a wind chill factor of ten zillion blogabits and at some point in time down the road there's a 40 per cent probability that we may experience some snow flurry activity.

Poor Robin stuck his head under his wing. We should be so lucky. What falls from the sky is much easier to escape than the blizzard of gibberish that beats around our heads year-round.

Our tormentors are many and various but, in these parts, what better month than March to focus our ire and vent our spleen on the weatherman. Here's a messenger for the shooting. Let's declare March "Don't Kick Pussy in the Guts Month" and spend the gratification thus diverted on the meteorologists.

At any rate, March is a month when bile is as high as energy is low. If we try to attack all the bafflegabbers on a broad front we'll just end up sputtering and fluttering on the floor like an untied balloon. No, let us concentrate and the weather person may come out of March all the better for it.

Politicians we'll set on the back burner until, say, September. Their gibberish is more amusing than harmful. They get 30 seconds on TV and their frantic efforts to make continuous sounds come out of their mouths is crude entertainment to the rest of us.

And the professions can wait. Lawyers, doctors, priests. Latin used to be the secret code language by which they excluded the great unwashed and by which they kept their self-esteem and their bills high. Bafflegab now is.

At any rate, our lawyers are now more or less incoherent with you at the fresh prospects held out to them by Canada's new constitution and Bill of Rights.

And priests, nowadays, have switched from Latin to sincere meaningful relevancies and from the nunc dimittis to a pro-or-con type situation vis-a-vis secular humanism. Jesus may still love them but many of their parishioners are running short of Christian charity.

Doctors, too, have forsaken Latin and even the petrifying "uh huh, uh huh" in favor of ECGs, EKGs, Catscans, "blood work" and "there's a lot of it going around." Tattoo your MCP number on the leg that doesn't need to come off and they'll seldom amputate the wrong one.

Neither should we squander our lowered energies in March on trying to back-track to the fountainhead of all gibberish.

John Dean and his Watergate chums get a lot of blame for the current wave of bastardized English. Some say that had yellow ribbons been tied firmly around their throats we would never have arrived at this point in time. But they certainly weren't the original sinners.

Years before that, there was a whole army of hacks, hucksters and petty bureaucrats inventing a secret language of gibberish and puffery like ersatz Masons. I think they have an underground college where they take lessons. And the filthy brutes attack us any hour of the night or day.

A digression but an example: This very morning I woke to hear a person on the radio say that "at some point in time down the road historically, we don't want to experience a Come-by-Chance-type situation."

Early as it was, my ears pricked. A few years ago I "experienced a Come-by-Chance-type situation" myself and have no fault whatsoever with it. I was born there.

So who was this joker bad-mouthing my natal seat? He was a gas-and-oil man who didn't want a repeat of the poor planning which helped to scupper an oil refinery at Come By Chance. He holds a doctorate in bafflegab.

But, to cleave to our resolve and take a fine bead through the jungle underbrush at the weatherman, what made him the gibbering, unlovely treacherous person he is today?

His empty patter can kill people or, at least, keep those with lower back pains awake at night under the threat of the snow-shovel.

He's spawned a silly lingo which is nation-wide and devilishly contagious. On any Royal or Papal tour you'll hear TV announcers from coast to coast say, "we're currently experiencing some rain-shower activity." They're telling the sight-impaired (formerly, the blind) that it's raining.

In the beginning there was Dr. Chase's Almanack and Uncle Albert's lumbago. Now there are satellites by which the milk bottles on Mr. Gorbachev's front porch may be counted. I don't know about your lot but ours would do better to consult Uncle Albert's joints.

For a short time we did enjoy the benefits of modern technology. American TV came here through Bangor, Maine. They'd show the blodges clearly on a map and a day or two later those Yankee squalls would drop on our heads in Newfoundland.

Even now when our U.S. TV comes through Detroit, the American predictions are a little behind lumbago twinges but still far ahead of the Canadian meteorological farce.

Was Bangor snatched away so that troublesome Newfs would drown faster in gales? Might as well go the whole paranoid hog. The local announcements through Bangor — Ladies Auxiliaries' card parties in Dartmouth, Portland or St. John's East — had begun to create a curious sense of Eastern Seaboard community here which must have rotted Ottawa's socks.

Television has much to answer for. Too often, it tries to make an entertainment of the weather forecast. You get a buffoon wearing funny hats and acting like he's running the ring-toss booth in some third-rate carnival — a hideous insult when the water is so cold and your boat so small.

In a place like Canada, metric is damned demoralizing. Month after month of below-zero Celsius is somehow harder to endure. As if that wasn't enough, somebody had to invent the "wind-chill factor" which makes it seem enticing to polar bears even if there's mud underfoot.

Maybe folk in Fredericton or Truro are better served by their weatherpersons. Ours take cover behind gibberish and geography. They say the Island is stuck so far out in the ocean that they tend to lose track of storms.

Bilge! If they can count Russian milk bottles how can they misplace a hairy great splodge of weather 500 miles across? But they do — and to get the rights of it you still have to look out the window or prod Uncle Albert.

The wilder their mistakes the thicker the bumph: "There's a 60 per cent probability that sometime down the road we may experience some snow flurry activity turning at times to heavy-type accumulations if high winds from the north change to strong gusts from the east causing reduced visibilities and clearing periods when the sun comes up tomorrow."

It's enough to make you experience a dry heave situation.

I SEE IN '83 A WELL NAMED ALICE …

L ong before the coppers were put on the eyes of 1982, there were doleful warnings that 1983 might not be worth getting out of bed for.

Mr. Trudeau kicked many pacemakers into overdrive with his prediction of a hard, hard winter … compared, one supposes, to last, which was not exactly a pig feast in Bora-Bora before the white man came. In Newfoundland, Mr. Peckford's mini-budget boosted the cost of living again by another 45 cents a bottle.

But are we despondent? Nooooo! Do we despair? Nooooo! This year is going to be interesting, if not bright, in spots. I know because I've inherited some small ability to predict. My father can put away warts and my mother has the uncanny inability to put anyone to bed without supper. I also have a cousin who can make other peoples' silverware vanish.

Gazing ahead, then, we see that the Happy Province laid its usual claim to the first baby born in 1983. Little Petroleum Pelley, infant daughter of Burt and Irene Pelley of Nippers Harbour East, entered the world at two and a quarter minutes past midnight on New Year's Day.

She beat by a narrow margin two other infants born within half an hour of the New Year ….Xavier Roustabout Parsons, son of John and Marie Parsons, St. John's, and Hibernia Sweetapple, daughter of Ms. Isadora Sweetapple of Grand Falls.

As the gas and oil fever here continues to rise many patriotic parents are placing related names on their new offspring. At the same time, so many new wells have been reported on the Grand Banks that names are running short. Bob and Carol and Ted and Alice were capped in December and await production. There's an official scheme to name future wells Brian XXVII, Brian XXVIII ... and so forth.

In June, 1982, a royal commission was appointed to investigate why unemployment and poverty in Newfoundland seem to rise in direct proportion to the amount of oil and gas discovered. This February, the commission will present its interim report. It will report the discovery that the foot bone is connected to the ankle bone. Also, that all God's chillun got shoes ... and will then pack its traps for further hearings in Montego Bay.

In March, on the feast of the Annunciation of the BVM, Finance Minister John Collins will announce that all God's chillun got shoes and that shoes are a luxury like ciggies and booze.

Dr. Collins will illustrate this by sticking a bare foot into a snowdrift and saying "Aarrrgggggh!" and then sticking in a shod foot while remarking "Ummmmmmmm!" He'll announce a 150% surtax on boots and shoes. Fierce opposition will later cause the minister to modify this policy so that only the left boot or shoe will carry the tax.

Good news in mid-April. Resource ministers in eastern Canada are to report that the scourge of the spruce budworm has been completely eliminated by acid rain. For this valuable service, New Jersey will present the Atlantic provinces with a bill for $57.8 million.

On May 16, Mr. Trudeau will repeat his earlier statement that if Newfoundland wants to leave Confederation it is free to go. Immediately, in fact, if it doesn't want (1) Cape Breton as a protectorate, (2) 250,000 Sicilian immigrants, (3) a nuclear test site in Terra Nova Park or (4) him to resign tomorrow.

A herring will be sighted about six miles southeast of Cape Race on June 23. Since the herring was long thought to be extinct, this report will cause great excitement. Fishing craft from 23 nations will race toward the area and Canada, desperate to fill its herring quota for this year, will appeal for help to the Swedish Armed Forces.

Using techniques employed by the Swedes to hunt snooping Russian subs, the Canadian forces will lay depth charges and small nuclear devices to force the herring to show itself. A two-

and-a-half-month-search will bring forth nothing but half an eel, a used French letter and three Russian submarines. Subsequently, the federal minister of fisheries will resign to resume his old job of teaching ceramics class in Ste. Agathe des Petits Phoques.

Shortly before Labour Day, Ottawa will announce that Halifax is to receive one-third of the federal budget for 1984, all the firstborn of Prince Edward Island, 200,000 expense-paid fortnights on the Love Boat and a free recording of Justin Trudeau practising kung fu on his teddy bear — not sold in any stores. Whereas St. John's will get boo sucks in a brown paper bag ... nyah, nyah, nyah!

Premier Peckford will say, what odds, we've still got our pride although it is becoming something of a luxury. Finance Minister Collins will announce a 150% luxury tax on pride, sex and the use of four-letter words. Twenty-six more oil wells are found, forcing unemployment up to 83%.

In the week after Thanksgiving, the Newfoundland Royal Commission on the Economy meets the federal Royal Commission on the Economy. To underline a point in these trying times, the commissioners will entertain each other at a dinner of pizza and beer and will lodge on the less-dear south coast of Barbados. In a joint press conference they'll reveal that the leg bone may be connected to the knee bone.

Finance Minister Collins will attempt to introduce a surtax on the use of knee bones for other than bona fide religious purposes but will scrap the plan when his own are interfered with by a three-quarter-inch Black and Decker drill.

During the third week in Advent, Premier Peckford will appeal to Prime Minister Trudeau for Canadian Forces to help deal with unusually high spirits in Newfoundland. Confederation Building will have been blown up and three residents of New Bonaventure overheard muttering outside the post office about switching their vote to the Liberals. Prime Minister Trudeau will respond immediately by sending along the widow of a veteran of the First World War armed with two pounds of navy beans and a stout rubber band.

On Dec. 31, Premier J.R. Smallwood will announce a $10,000 prize to the first baby in 1984 who's got the makings of a damned fine Liberal.

All in all, not a superlative year, perhaps, but surely enough to keep the mind half alive.

AT LAST. SALT COD IS TRENDY

A chap I met in school in Toronto and whose dad owned most of the supermarkets in Jamaica once asked me if codfish had human faces.

Newfie jokes hadn't then been spawned, so I had no reflexive urge to alter his elegant dental work. Although he later dropped out of journalism school to take ballet lessons, he seemed to be as nimble in the attic as he was on his pins. No, he was being serious. Jamaicans saw only salt codfish, and because these arrived headless, the notion grew up among the more superstitious that cod had heads like people. I reassured him that even in a poor light you couldn't mistake a cod's head for that of John the Baptist or, come to that, Kirk Douglas.

King Cod. In Newfoundland, at least, the royal name was seldom spoken. If you said fish you meant cod, while the lesser breeds were called by name — salmon, herring, halibut. You went trouting in a brook with rod and line, never fishing.

In school when asked to draw a fish, we took the easy way out and sketched a dried cod — just a long triangle with tail attached but two scallops up top where the head had come off. The same appeared on a stamp with the legend "Newfoundland Currency" below it, and coins from St. Pierre of featherweight aluminum were stamped with the same curious triangle. For centuries these hard salted triangles had been shipped off by the millions to feed the slaves of the Caribbean, the poor of the Mediterranean, the natives of South America and the Catholics of Northern Europe.

Once when I was in Barbados and quite stewed by the sun and soused on Planter's Punch I got peevish about being called "honkey" or "ghost" once too often. There was an anti-white wave going through the West Indies at the time, much of it imported all of a piece from the States.

"Look here, chummy," I said to a taunting Bajan, having prudently selected an uncommonly small one, "I wonder who got the dirtier end of the stick — my great grandaddy or yours? Mine slaved like a black to send down saltfish to yours and neither saw a dollar from one year's end to the next. It was a vicious triangle which kept the sugar bowls of London full. Don't you dare tell me that my crowd trod on the necks of yours."

This pretty piece of philosophy seemed to have no effect on the chap, and as some huskier brethren were approaching, I remounted my Raleigh and pedalled for the next parish, pausing only to shout: "Those fish we send down do have faces like people."

It was only 20 years ago or less that frozen cod began to replace dried fish here. The switchover was fast and complete. Villages were cleared of the structures, trappings, outbuildings and equipment needed in the saltfishery, and now any landlubberly schoolboy could shove off in a rowboat and sell his catch to collectors on the beach.

"Too many people chasing too few fish," declared Ricky Cashin's new union. A crusade to weed out the moonlighters and shore up the bona fides began. Meanwhile, the Russians and other Europeans came along with factory ships which vacuumed everything off the Grand Banks except the rocks.

During the Smallwood years, the fishery was scorned in favour of rubber plants, chocolate factories and other exotica. However, a Fisheries College was started, and the man found to head it had invented that ultimate desecration of fish, the breaded, frozen fish stick.

Today, offshore gas and oil has pushed the fishery into a corner, and the current fisheries minister is worm-bored cabinet timber, indeed. On top of that, Ottawa sticks in its oar with all the gaffes and floundering that that usually entails.

Quality control is a scandal. No self-respecting Scandinavian dog would touch some of the stuff that comes out of Newfoundland fish plants. Workers have told me they've had to check out sick after retching and heaving half the day over a particular batch of fish.

Another disgrace, and one that occurs most summers, is that during the height of the cod season hundreds of tons are dumped or left to rot because the plants can't handle them. A complication this year is that the Japanese have discovered capelin — particularly the roe of the hen capelin — thought to transform honourable but flagging grandfathers into raging satyrs. The demand and price for this piscatorial equivalent of rhinoceros horn is such that some plants turn away cod in favor of capelin.

Which brings us right back around again to the salt cod industry. Even Fisheries Minister James ("Dim") Morgan now opines that salted dried cod would be a viable way to handle the glut. Because saltfish is no longer cheap fodder for slaves and peasants. Trendy amateur chefs in America, for instance, are informed by culinary gurus like Beard, Child and Claiborne that Morue Portugaise is one in the eye for the Joneses and that Brandade de Morue will get them lionized in Wichita.

Beard says his favourite codfish dishes are based on the salt cod and gives assembly instructions for the stuff done in the Armenian, Spanish, Lyonnaise, Carcassone, Marseillaise and cod knows how many other styles. (He seems to have overlooked Morue à la Bung Hole Tickle, which is salt cod wrapped in layers of well-wetted newspaper, then chucked into the midst of a wood fire ... and a wonderful grand grog-bit it is, too, of a frosty winter's night.)

But the hitch is that when all these chic U.S. kitchens commence clamouring for salt cod it'll have to be imported from Norway. Not many here now know or remember how to make it. The necessary paraphernalia has been destroyed. Under the old system, large families and much labour were required.

The practice probably lasted longer in Newfoundland than in the other Atlantic provinces. In my teens, 25 years ago, the adolescent dream of sailing off to Trinidad or Rio or Cadiz or Naples in a schooner laden with saltfish was still a real possibility. But the markets faded abroad and, at home, the drudgeries and failures of the past were used to scupper any notion of a salt cod fishery of the future and to underline the joys and prosperity of aluminum smelters to come.

For all that, there may still be some hope. We've got to do something until the time comes when we'll be up to the hips in oily Rollses, Lear jets, manor houses, great gobs of emeralds and you.

"Making" salt cod is as complicated as producing cheese or wine, but surely a small pool of expertise still exists. New gadgets and techniques must now be available to take some of the drudgery out of the job. The thousands of women and children who stand like robots in chilly, reeking fish plants might be glad of a choice. From the consumer's end of it, if I had to choose between good saltfish and those breaded, frozen fish sticks, I would hesitate no longer than a U.S. Congressman faced with a pensionable Water Street tart and Raquel Welch.

Speaking of which ... if Dim Morgan would only spread the word of the Japanese discovery about capelin eggs around the chic environs of Washington, D.C., we need never fear for the future. Trudeau, MacEachen and the boys might then seize all our offshore petroleum and put it to whatever ends they saw fit ... and be damned to them all.

CURSE HIBERNIA! IT KILLED THE GOOD OLD POVERTY SCAM

Hibernia is playing hell with my old lifestyle. It's making me stinking rich and I don't think I can handle that. This is an attempt, futile, I dare say, to save myself.

If everyone else here had the same problem I think I could live with it. But among more fortunate Newfoundlanders proud poverty and carefree unemployment are actually on the upswing, God be praised. Even Crosbie enterprises have had some reverses.

That, you might think, is rather like a harp repair shop in heaven going knockers up. Not so. Mainlanders are getting an imperfect picture of recent events here in the Happy Province.

That's because their press, inflamed by itself and the extravagant attitudes put around by Mr. Peckford, has us all prematurely rolling around like swine in excrement in the filthy riches of gas and oil.

But quaint and contented poverty is still the general ticket. The only group to be swamped so far by Hibernian wealth is we handful of local freelance journalists. The mainland press, mad keen to have its audience know what it's like to have stinking riches for all descend on Newfoundland, have encumbered us with a steady shower of scandalously large cheques in return for the luscious details.

It's got to stop. In the vain hope of forestalling fresh embarrassments of riches from *The Globe and Mail, Maclean's* magazine, the CBC and the rest of them, I've decided to set down the standard questions and answers here, once and for all:

QUESTION: *Now that you, a typical Newfie, have been indirectly made stinking rich by Hibernia, what's it really like?*

ANSWER: I foresee a bleak future for Newfoundland if gas and oil means that everyone else here eventually wallows in luxury as I already do. As one of the handful who have truly prospered (in a roundabout way) through the discoveries in Iceberg Alley, I find I have come too far, too fast. My personality has altered and my old friends shun me, both of them. Even though I can now afford weekly baths in hot water.

QUESTION: *What's the biggest heart-ache involved in being jerked from the mire of abject poverty, the natural state of all Newfies, to the heady pinnacle of petroleum pasha?*

ANSWER: Indubitably, the suffering of the children. They're now jeered or avoided on the playground because the patches on their clothing are put on with smaller and neater stitches than are those on the garments of their little playmates. Their mother is accused of being able to loll around at home in squalid luxury with more time to waste on the patching.

QUESTION: *You, as bellwether and guinea pig of the staggering wealth soon to afflict the rest of your countrymen, say the path to true happiness lies elsewhere?*

ANSWER: You are damned tooting. In the dirt-poor but happy days of yore all we had to peddle abroad was pickled herring and our poverty, and a pleasant little racket it was, too. Poverty is a self-renewing resource. For instance, from one year's end to the next, *Today* magazine might pester me only once — and that around the Yuletide for reminiscences of poverty-stricken yet quaint and merry Christmases in Newfoundland.

Thus was I kept poverty-stricken and my reminiscences were all the more keen and poignant for it. All us artistes had a fine old time of it painting, singing and writing about the grinding poverty of Newfoundland, yet remained in no danger of losing our status thereby. Now, "Newfpov" goes begging for markets on the mainland because no one there believes it exists anymore.

Instead, there are crippling fortunes to be made these days by telling outsiders how oil-crazed and wealthy we're all supposed to have become.

QUESTION: *Why do Newfies, once the most docile and deferential race that ever trod shoe leather down at the heel, now hate mainlanders' guts?*

ANSWER: Because mainlanders now hate our guts for being stinking rich and oil-crazed, which, since we're not, is hateful. If you follow. Yet the stinking-rich-already theory is the only one the mainland media'll buy, so ...

QUESTION: *Into what do you plow your own stinking riches?*

ANSWER: Gin and medical advice.

QUESTION: *Have you ever thought of getting a second opinion? How widely are mainland guts hated in Newfie?*

ANSWER: Strictly speaking, it is Ontario that is the Great Satan. Cape Bretoners have never called us "nigger," if only out of consideration for the black race. I would say that roughly three-quarters of the households in Newfoundland today have a jar of formaldehyde on the mantelpiece in which are several feet of guaranteed mainland intestine.

In fact, they are processed by a factory in Quebec and once belonged to Newfoundland ponies shipped there for the pot. And, no, if you want a feature article on that at special rates from me, I'm already dickering with Walt Disney Inc.

These jars of ersatz mainland viscera are glowered at hatefully before meals and in more orthodox families also in the morning and before bedtime.

QUESTION: *Is the shortage of Mercedes and Rolls mechanics the most appalling problem facing Newfoundland today?*

ANSWER: Not since the week before last when a fresh shipload arrived, mostly the younger sons of sheiks.

QUESTION: *What have you done personally in an attempt to shake off the curse of premature Hibernian stinking riches?*

ANSWER: I offered to burn my ACTRA card on national TV, but ACTRA cautioned me that I'd have to accept supra-special rates for the performance. I've tried to donate my Writer's Union membership to a worthy cause like Farley Mowat, but Saturday Night threatened to commission a first-person account of it. Global television wants a script dealing with my real-life tragedy and, damned albatross, who better for the starring role?

QUESTION: *Will you scatter the ludicrously inflated fee for this article among your fellow Newfies as a help to preparing themselves to meet the anguish of untold riches soon to befall them?*

ANSWER: Hell, no. I wouldn't wish the suffocating burden of that on any old dog, let alone Newfoundland ones.

NEW NEWFOUNDLAND: "ABSOLUTELY DISGUSTING"

With our first gas-and-oil billions we really must hop right out and buy ourselves a Canary. Or an Azore, or a housebroken Antille. It's high time we had some balmy adjunct in which we might escape the vernal excesses of the northwest Atlantic. April blizzards were always hard to take but now they're mixed with the chilling slush of Canadian sanctimony.

We need the break. A toasty isle must go at the top of our shopping list. I can see us now ... keeled off on our own Canary, eating scrambled Fabergé eggs for breakfast, being fetched pineapplesful of iced Screech by former directors of Air Canada. Ahhh. Four centuries wasn't long to wait. All we had to do was fear God, honour the King and wait until our ship came in.

We are going to be absolutely disgusting. Here comes Jack with his three years' pay! There won't be a single unrevolted puritanical set of guts in all of Upper Canada. I think I've heard my first dry heave already. A fellow from a Toronto magazine rang me up the other day and asked how Newfoundlanders were handling their guilt. What guilt was he talking about?

"Most Canadians think Newfoundlanders are being greedy," said he. "Doesn't that make them feel guilty? How are they handling it? With the usual wit, humour and booze?"

"Naw, bye," I said, lapsing into the requisite lingo. "Shure, the money is made for to go 'round. When 'tis all gone, what odds? We'll have all the enjoyment squeezed out of it and that's the main t'ing."

I heard a faint sound like a sculpin being squeezed to death in a presbyter's armpit. They expect us, you see, to pass all the loot over to those who are trained to handle the filthy stuff without becoming polluted. In other words, them. But they'll never shame it out of us. Newfoundlanders most certainly are not greedy. Even in our normal state — that is to say, poverty-stricken — we were always generous.

I remember my own granny, night after night, working her poor scurvied fingers to the bone knitting bedsocks for Asia's starving millions. Or my grandpa, his little berri-berried knees scarce able to support him, canvassing the village for toothbrush-kits to ship off to Africa's teeming destitute so that they might at least maintain the equipment with which they worried their toasted locust larvae.

Great God in Heaven! We, ungenerous? Shall not the same race which gave — that the poor Hottentot might enjoy his shish-ka-bug — also contribute lest the microwave ovens of Etobicoke grow dim or the Cuisinarts of Scarborough grind slow? Ours'll be the first hand into the back pocket when the cry goes out on behalf of the boat people of Richelieu Manor or Mrs. Fred Davis does a telethon in aid of Rosedale poodle clinics.

During the late Campaigns Mr. Trudeau passed among us on a guilt-mongering foray. Miserable wretches, during the 30 years of Confederation had we not been in receipt of $6 billion in Canadian charity? Yet, now we could clasp those undersea riches to our parsimonious bosoms. Thus spake the gunslinging collector for the Cross-Canada Credit Bureau. Would he dump the baby into the ditch and chuck the repossessed perambulator into the back of his van? Not this time ... but he would return.

We had the guilt laid on us, and then the threat. Disco Daddy did the Petro CanCan. Without a federal Godfather to our backs, Newfoundlanders would be rooked, bilked, deked and diddled by the petro-megacorps. In short, if God had not meant us to be fleeced he would not have made us so woolly.

Our great Imperial dream of getting our hooks on a Canary dimmed. On the one hand prowled a ravenous Exxon and, on the other, lurked Trudeau's Ottawa, handmaiden of — and purveyor to — an insatiable Ontario and Quebec. We were doomed, as usual, to the unhygienic end of the stick.

But hist! List! Pssst! Out of the gloom when all seemed lost bounced mettlesome young Alfie Peckford. He grasped that selfsame stick and raised it aloft with a new Newfoundland flag billowing from the top of it. Needless to say, this will completely defuse Ottawa. Federal pressure will be lifted from us. We'll be free to take our better chances with the megacorps. For the terrible threat to central Canada was not the chance of freezing in the dark. It was a far more terrible spectre. That of 500,000 persons carousing about the globe, committing the most appalling gaucheries and plastered fore and aft with Maple Leaves.

Now that we're getting our own emblem to stitch on our outer garments and affix to our traps and baggage, the precious National Identity of Canada abroad will be spared the horrendous besmirching that Ottawa could never hope to repair, not even by smuggling 600 Republicans out of New Jersey.

Clever Alfie! There's the deal which gets the feds off our backs. They'll let us keep Hibernia if we'll do our guilt-free un-Canadian roistering under our own colours. Now, then: "Wanted to Buy — One medium-sized Canary, all mod. cons., southn. exposr., bathrooms optional. Apply to 500,000 of God's ragamuffin children who have waited 400 years for a place in the sun." When we have first brightened the corner where we are, alms-box-shaking will be wholeheartedly entertained. As ever, Granny could have told you that.

THE NEW NEWFOUNDLAND CHAUVINISM? IT'S RIDICULOUS

Have a glass of our lovely Newfoundland water," says the lady of the house to the visiting Toronto journalist. "Better than your old mainland water. 'Tis a lot wetter." That sketch by the local satirical group, CODCO, collided with reality this summer when a medical researcher at Memorial University claimed that Newfoundland water, "the softest in North America," may cause stomach cancer. He said the water may react chemically with plumbing, giving the island four times the Continental rate of that affliction.

CODCO, to stay in the vanguard of comic exaggeration, will have to knock out a skit next in which a great wave of tumour-pride has swept Newfoundland, one full of black jokes about chauvinistic carcinoma. Even that wouldn't be too far fetched. There's been a violent swing of the pendulum here from abject grovelling to aggressive strutting. One of these ridiculous extremes is just as loathsome and as eminently mockable as the other.

"Oil fever," is the instant diagnosis of Upper Canada. Not true. The swing away from forelock-tugging, foot-shuffling and a please-kick-me-again attitude began long before Ben Nevis and Hibernia were even whispered about. Newfoundlanders used to have a great inferiority complex. It would take a historian to tell you what spawned and nurtured it. Centuries of colonial rule and economic helplessness must have played their parts.

The drift toward belligerent xenophobia began in the late Fifties when 20-year-olds discovered that, despite the Smallwoodian hype and monumental puffery about the blessings of Confederation, there was no future for them in Newfoundland. They went down the road at the rate of 10,000 and more a year, disillusioned by the exaggerated promises of Confederation and defeated by the great Newfoundland puzzle of why 156,000 square miles (above water) could not even support a population the size of a small city. They took with them the dismal litany of Newfoundland superlatives — highest cost of living, lowest wages, highest unemployment, lowest rate of literacy, highest provincial taxes, lowest standard of health.

The human flow out of the province continued. To and past Toronto to Alberta and the Pacific coast. By the end of the 1960s there were enough Newfoundlanders scattered across the continent to be noticeable and it was noticed that they were somehow "different". Hence, Newfie jokes. Even though he was excessively modest and preconditioned to kowtow, the Newfoundlander found this wasn't enough. He came from a godforsaken rock somewhere off the west coast of Greenland, inhabited by incestuous idiots and drunken cretins, a bottomless pit into which the poor, overburdened Canadian Taxpayer poured billions in welfare in return for a few lousy fiddle tunes.

It was somewhere along this trail that the worm commenced to turn. At home in Newfoundland and especially among the new upper middle class of St. John's there grew up the Wetter Water Brigade. A frantic search was mounted for any remaining bits and scraps of "pure Newfoundlandia." Fiddlers and storytellers and primitive artists and even plain old salts of the earth were declared national treasures, yanked out of their rustic cul-de-sacs and lashed through their paces at a killing clip.

Young professionals who'd been boarding-schooled and universitied at great expense abroad suddenly lapsed back into the broadest and most incomprehensible of outport accents and wore fishermen's sweaters to the best urban cocktail parties. Old and honest bits of buffoonery, curious scraps of tradition, half-forgotten quirks and customs were seized upon and magnified and glorified by the Wetter-Water Brigade.

Thus the seal hunt was elevated from the status of a simple bit of outdoor butchery to some sort of folk-religion, a vital tradition, a quasi-spiritual exercise without which all our souls would be damned forever to those regions where the water is merely moist. It was long before offshore oil and gas that the silly excesses of Brian Davies and Greenpeace produced a reaction from some Newfoundlanders that was just as foolish and excessive.

That same defensive reaction to any real or imagined criticism or slight or threat wafting down the Gulf of St. Lawrence has snowballed. The dimmest of our politicians — let alone Brian Peckford — can now latch on to it and be as secure of waxing fat as a maggot lodged in the carcass of a beached whale. Even a native son has got to think twice these days before he questions the desperate sort of patriotism that has given us the lightest air, the hardest rocks and the wettest water in the world.

Two of my native son acquaintances, home on visits from Toronto this summer, did so in a mild way and were invited to hightail it back to either Commanis Chiner or Commanis Rusher or Etobicoke, where they belonged. One of them had protested against being fiddled and folksonged and squeeze-boxed and jigged and wetter-watered to death in St. John's (and that in public places!) while the other had complained, after a solid fortnight of rain, drizzle and fog, that the weather stank. Two Newfoundlanders, at least, who found the old jokes easier to take than the new Newfies.

OF TRAVEL AND TRADES

AN INNOCENT ABROAD

It was April, not February, but chunks of ice still bobbed about in the harbour, and there were six inches of slush on the road. The fisherman next door came by as I was pitching towels, sun tan oil and swim fins into the trunk of the dark green Corvair.

"What the devil are you going at with that?" he said.

"I'm going to take it somewhere I can use it," I replied with a show of counterfeit bravado. For the next six weeks that odd combination of terror and exhilaration stayed with me. Come By Chance to Key West and back by way of Expo '67.

I spent most of one day trying to escape from Boston. They have a tunnel under the harbour, the first one I'd ever driven. The speed limit was 45 m.p.h., but the closeness of the walls make it seem more like 90. I touched the brakes which caused the monstrous truck on my rear bumper to blast its air horn and I think my eyes squirted blood.

But being trapped in a circle in Boston was no more daunting than the blizzard in the middle of Newfoundland. There were no houses in 100 miles, and when the whiteout came down you might as well have been buried alive. The gulf ferry ploughed through ice most of the way to North Sydney.

In New Brunswick, it was floods. Traffic was rerouted to increasingly narrower roads, and when I got to the Maine border I ran out of road map. That's when I discovered that all Americans don't talk like TV announcers.

I couldn't understand the guy at the service station at all. He said "whup" a lot, which I figured later to be "yes," and he made much reference to something called "innostayed" — the Interstate — and I ended up that evening blundering around the pine woods on the fringe of a military base, and the warning signs were horrendous.

The last thing I wanted to do was run afoul of GI Joe because I'd been roughly treated by a U.S. customs gent earlier in the day. My own silly fault. He asked the purpose of the trip and I said I was escaping the draft ... "the cold Canadian draft, heh, heh."

You don't joke with those birds. He commenced heaving his questions at me over and over again, round about, back to front and I thought I'd be handed over next to Efrem Zimbalist Jr. This jaunt doesn't sound like a whole bunch of chuckles so far, but the relief after these bouts of terror was exquisite.

Your mainland lad is quite used, I dare say, to border crossings, Interstates and U.S. accents, but at that time in Newfoundland, the only highway was two lanes wide, and there was a single highway overpass. I was green, a very pale green, half the time.

But finally I blundered into Bangor, bought a road atlas, and settled down for the night. Colour television, key lime pie, red-white-and-blue mailboxes — all neat stuff that you didn't get in Come By Chance.

Years before, my mother had passed through the customs sheds of Ellis Island and now I know exactly what she meant about that mixture of excitement and intimidation felt by immigrants to the great new land.

Discovering from my new maps about beltways didn't save me from the horrors of Boston, and so great was my dread of New York that I cut around it about 100 miles to the west. This didn't deliver me from a rush hour in New Jersey with 10 lanes of traffic belting along cheek by jowl. Water Street would hold no terrors after this.

It got warmer and the trees began to leaf out as in slow motion film. By Washington, it was summer. The few famous sites I've been able to compare with their pictures have one thing in common: the litter doesn't show in the pictures. The reflecting pool in front of the Lincoln Memorial was chock-a-block with rubbish, which struck me as odd since the Yanks seem so fastidious in their personal habits. Pictures often lie, though. I hadn't expected those appalling slums within blocks of the famous buildings.

As I was walking down the zillion or so steps in the Washington Monument there came a thunderous roar from above which grew closer. A joint shudder of fear ran through the tourists around me, who were mostly elderly whites, as a gang of black youths ran past, knocking all from their path.

Perhaps TV has reinforced our expectations of a brutal side of America. In Georgia I detoured on a red dirt road and looked back to find a convertible with a Confederate flag and full of red-neck louts close to my rear bumper. They yelled and jeered, and it was a tense 10 miles before they stopped their sport.

And as I was about to enter a restaurant in Scranton, Pa., out burst five men in black hats and coats and dark glasses. The way the other citizens flattened themselves against the building as they swept past made me doubt that they were Sunday School teachers.

You meet your better sort of stereotypes, too. One night on a Florida campground I woke to find my airmattress floating in two feet of water. It was a flash flood. In an adjacent plot an aged granny had been left in charge of five grandchildren. Lordy, but she was feisty! She had those kids rounded up and bundled off to the high ground while the rest of us were still splashing around in panic. It was no trouble to picture her going west in a covered wagon picking arrows out of her poke bonnet.

With three or four of life's niftier experiences your First Time is likely to be unforgettable. So it was with my first glimpse of a sub-tropical sea. Just outside Jacksonville, I scrambled and slipped up the side of a white sand dune, and then I started to laugh like a maniac.

That colour was impossible. Here was a whole ocean of that same blazing turquoise you get in swimming pools. I'd thought the tropical sea in pictures was a trick of light and film and that the real thing could never be so brilliant. Some people on the beach paid no attention as I galloped down the sand and into the sea, clothes and all. Winter-crazed northerners are no novelty here. It's only April, I kept thinking. Only April.

Some books are like that. You're sorry to have read *Huckle-berry Finn* or *Boswell's Johnson* for the first time because you'll never be able to have that sublime experience again. When the tires spin and the nose drips and the furnace goes into overdrive, the sustaining flashback I get is that first glimpse of Florida's unearthly water.

I reversed the film and backtracked into spring again at Montreal. Expo '67 was rather different from Come By Chance, too, but I found the biggest thrill in town to be the traffic. At least in Boston they keep their hands on the steering wheel while they scream at you. And so to home. Still plenty of ice in the Cabot Strait and a respectable little snowflurry as I rolled ashore at Port aux Basques, and the trees were still bare. After all, it was only the first week in June.

COLUMNIST WRITES STAGE PLAY, BECOMES WARPED FOR LIFE

A nd so to bed, sick of life," was a common whine of diarist Samuel Pepys.

So it is with freelance writers. It's an uneven way of life. Jobs come either in thick bunches or they don't come at all.

Whether it's feast or famine it's hard on the nerves. Sitting around flinging shoes at the cat is every bit as strenuous as thinking up ways to mollify six editors at once when their deadlines have whizzed past like express boxcars. One side effect of this strain is that you come to have the personality of a porcupine with ingrown quills.

For all that, there's no better job. It's never dull and there are always surprises. You take, for instance, "Triff the Stiff."

That's my short title for a stage play I wrote this spring: *Young Triffie's Been Made Away With*. The body of young Tryphenia Maude Pottle, retarded daughter of the maniacal Pastor William Henry Pottle is found on the beach by ... et cetera.

It was my first experience. A wonderful one it was, too. While it lasted there was no going "to bed, sick of life."

Atlantic Insight made mention of this threat to W. Shakespeare in the May issue. It's curious how your own hype comes back to haunt you. My wife does consume a fair number of trashy novels ... "the ruination of a once-fine mind," I tell her ... but this wasn't really my first inspiration.

Money was. A group of local artistes somehow scraped together enough money to do a freshly-written play. As we went along, I caught a hint of how hard and soul-sickening it is these days to dredge up money for "the arts."

All the tales of woe you've heard in recent months are true. The Mulroney administration's massacre of arts and culture funds is as deadly as Agent Orange. There was waste and frivolity and self-indulgence under the old system but now I fear we'll see formula pap.

One good thing, though, about being a freelancer in Newfoundland — or for that matter, Atlantic Canada — is that you must be prepared to do wild and weird things.

If the market here was bigger and broader there are those of us who would never dream of attempting a play or ghost-writing some old codger's memoirs or doing a commercial about "burning rectal itch."

But here, with a pile of bills the chief incentive, we take a snap at almost anything.

School janitors in this area nearly did in "Triff the Stiff" for the second time. About 100 of them went on strike which put about 12,000 students out of school for nearly three weeks ... our two blessings included. I would bawl at them to get outdoors and play hopscotch in a blizzard and then heave the typewriter at the cat.

"Parenting" chez Guy hasn't been the same since. I would try out "Triff the Stiff" lines by roaring out things like "You Witch of Endor, you a**-licker of Satan, you fornicating jezebel ... " and it became increasingly difficult to prise the little dears from under the bed.

"Triff" also helped me to my first stomach ulcer. You think editors are the only ones who ride you about trifles like deadlines? Compared to stage producers they are but Gandhi to Himmler.

Medication, both pharmaceutical and bottled-in-bond, got me through. But some combination of pills and/or substances struck me damn nigh dumb on the very day a Montreal movie producer asked me out to lunch. I sounded like a gramophone with a sprung mainspring and dammit, I suppose now the Oscar will have to wait.

First night is a thousand deaths for scriveners of stage plays. Suppose the audience laughs at the wrong bits ... or not at all. I missed my opening by the simple means of taking aboard so much Dutch Courage as to be rendered horizontal.

"Well received," reported the local critics going on to say that the dialogue was adequate but the plot was nowhere in sight and the structure nonexistent.

There was no news of rotten eggs or vegetation being flung so next night I trotted along myself.

Cashews who choose to write for a living meet various reactions, depending on the medium. A piece in a newspaper might get you a few letters the next day, in magazines the next month, in books or TV, the next year. But nothing increases the size of your head like the stage.

Reaction, good or bad, is visible, audible and immediate. Exactly that many people are groaning, hooting, laughing or applauding. You think, "OK, ladies and gents, get ready for another dashed good giggle in exactly 8.5 seconds," and it happens. It could warp you for life.

It's gratifying, too, because you can see that even a scribbler does his bit for the economy, for society. He has helped create this much entertainment, this much employment for this many people, has caused this much cash to be turned over. Freelancers sometimes feel they're at the bottom of the heap. Here is a cure.

In my own case it was a cure also for middle-age madness. I got caught up in a few revelries with the youthful (compared to pudge-gut pappy, here) artistes. Downtown St. John's might not be the Vienna Woods but a few nights of it nearly put me under with Young Triffy.

Something of all this must be what keeps going those connected with the stage. It's a gruelling life and it pays peanuts. Politicians who would cut their meagre dole are the sort that kick over baby carriages for recreation.

Meanwhile, I've caught the stage bug. I may do what the big boys do, write a sequel, "Triffy II." Ah, yes, Young Triff was not really made away with ... that was her long-lost twin sister.

It's five years later, the mad Pastor's been sprung from the lunatic asylum and another rash of dead and mutilated sheep breaks out over the once-peaceful Swyers Harbour.

Was the Pastor sprung too early or does this mean that the troubled war veteran, Vincy Bishop, has returned from New Zealand to where he bolted from the law in 1947? And what of the law? Is it true that the stalwart Ranger Hepditch has turned to politics and has joined the rest in plundering the public chest? Did Mrs. Melrose really succumb to a massive dose of morphine? Was Billy Head really the innocent youth of nature? Will aunt Milly Bishop and old man Washbourne actually ... ?

I can see it now. Albums, T-shirts, videos, screen adaptations, paperbacks, kiddie spinoffs. Young Triffie goes to Hollywood, that sort of thing.

J.B. sweetheart, can we take a lunch on Friday?

RIDING THE DEAD SKUNK TRAIL

It smells just like hot chocolate," said the younger passenger in the back seat, "sort of mixed up with strong, strong, garlic!"

No, my first act ashore was not to barf all over Cape Breton. My tripes held firm despite the grisly description and the odour it identified. All the more miraculous because I'd not long before attempted a CN ferry breakfast.

Dead Skunk is what it was. The children were enchanted. For miles they groaned and yucked and practised pseudo retching. Poor deprived tots, they never see a skunk, alive or defunct, in Newfoundland. There aren't any ... or porcupines or raccoons.

If the Nova Scotia tourist board was on its toes it would promote dead skunks to the skies as a lure to juvenile Newfoundlanders of a certain age. They can get all the Peggy's Coves they want at home. With a deceased skunk brought back in a baggie they'd lord it over their little neighbours for weeks.

Backtracking slightly, the CN ferry still compares badly with the Onassis yacht. The crew, for the most part, are friendly and helpful but there are drawbacks. Food, for instance. "Take the half grapefruit and the rice krispies, dear," advised the kindly tourist from New Jersey. "They can't do anything to that."

I was about to offer her odds of ten-to-one but thought better of it. The bacon was cold and congealed, the eggs were somehow plasticized and the toast better-suited to skimming across a calm marine surface. And the cafeteria lineups can be fierce ... 80 or 90 to a queue with hungry howling infants spaced along it.

If luck is with you there'll be a raging gale, three parts of the other passengers will be in their bunks praying for a merciful release and, if you put a reef knot in your bowels, you can have the caf to yourself and the food before it has started to mould.

We were following the Dead Skunk Trail to the Laurentians. We tried to ease the pain of steerage by dawdling. A few hundred miles a day and a safe haven and some nourishing gin at the end of it. For instance, at New Glasgow we departed the truck-ridden Trans-Canada Highway and took to a byway along the Northumberland Strait prettily named the Sunrise Trail. It was a vast improvement both to the nerves and to the vision. Nothing can tranquillize you faster than a Nova Scotia cow slumped peacefully in her tracks in the green grass beside the azure sea. It was a great temptation to stop right here in Cow Dung County and go no further.

Drivers along the route have, according to the region, different styles, attitudes and various levels of indifference as to when they embrace eternity.

In Cape Breton, a certain highland bloodthirstiness mixed with suicidal Gaelic élan greets the fear-crazed Newfoundlander used, on home turf, only to motoring atrocities at much slower speeds.

You get more of your Presbyterian caution in Nova Scotia proper except for the bullying transport trucks in transit which are a constant reminder anywhere that you haven't put your immortal soul in order.

Slow is more the rule in New Brunswick. Much of the rural traffic gives only an approximation of motion. The rule here is for the transient eager beaver to come up to within inches of the local slowpoke and crack his nerve by blaring horn, flashing light and various other menaces thus forcing him off the road.

Quebec? Best to grip the wheel, put down your foot and shut your eyes until it's over. There's something about a rear bumper that enrages your Québecois to the point of lunacy.

Each and every one of them has the God-given compulsion to pass the rear bumper ahead or perish gloriously in the attempt. But he that is passed then has the same sacred trust to do likewise so that by the time Quebec traffic reaches the Ontario border it is hurtling along at Mach 5.

In a once-tranquil part of Montreal West the Curse of the Pit Bull Terrier had struck. Some ruffian from beyond the borders of that suburb had brought his hell-hound into a small corner park. It had playfully gnashed the heavy plastic swing seats to tatters. There was a great flurry and shouting as parents scrambled their tiny tots behind doors and, too late, came the police.

There was an exchange of grisly details from verandas and over back fences: whereas a German Shepherd could exert a jaw pressure of a mere 800 pounds, the pit bull was capable of 1,500; it attacked anything that moved; it was used as a deadly weapon in robberies; druggies preferred it to the sub-machine gun ... the brute's charms were seemingly endless.

And so we left terror-stricken Montreal West for the peaceful Laurentians. We might as well have stayed home ... if scenery was the only consideration. Down to the last hill, tree, bush and pond the area we saw was almost exactly like Thorbourned Lake or Deer Lake. End of comparison. Here, the "cottages" have ten bedrooms each, hot tubs, saunas, swimming pools, tennis courts, water skiing, wind surfing, sailing, motor boats, servants.

Hogsheads of ready cash can do nothing with the weather, though, and here as eastward to North Sydney there was moaning about a filthy summer. "Worst in 30 years" was the popular estimate although some were prepared to go to 50 and 60. One distraught farmer in New Brunswick took it back to the Acadian Expulsion.

If you don't take orderly notes, the memories of a travelling holiday tend to be like the crazy quilts sold in every self- respecting hamlet and bus stop in the Maritimes. Orderly anything is not my idea of a holiday. This one was a great success, it being about as orderly as the back seat of the car after the youngsters had occupied it for three days running.

Some things stand out vividly among the jumble. The apocalyptic horror of crossing a Montreal bridge at rush hour on Friday afternoon; the children's delight at small non-Newfoundland things like squirrels and square stop lights; the kindness and "lack of side" of people who own ten-bedroom summer shacks.

Then there was the surprising milky-blueness of a calm Cabot Strait in the early morning; the affinity with some New Brunswick Acadians we met; the rush to see how the cats and the garden had done when we landed back home once more.

A big hit with the kinder was Antigonish for its physical beauty but much more for the name itself. When they first heard it pronounced they whooped and screeched like a pair of zanys and after various alterations settled on "Auntie-go-squish." Then they incorporated all their various aunties and pounded the living heck out of the "joke" for the next 200 miles.

At the 208th mile, both parents cracked at once and in unison issued a loud and savage protest. Much good it did. After a brief sulk they decided to nickname us "Dud" and "Mud" and so it remains until this very day.

FLOOSHING THE
FARINACEOUS MIND

W riter's block is one name for the hideous condition. Mental constipation is another. Dry heaves is one of the more pleasant symptoms.

To make a comparison: there's a Newfie Bullet joke (not my own) about a young fellow who takes his first train trip and gets violently sick.

Says a kindly conductor, "Don't worry, my boy, nobody yet has died of motion sickness."

Replies the lad, "To hell with that. The hope of death is all that's keeping me alive right now."

Writer's block is rather like that. You can't get off the train until it gets to your station and that depot is the last word on the last page. Your brain is farinaceous, your eyes glazed in panic and your fingers locked into rigid hooks.

Writer's spouses, if they're halfway clever (which is unlikely since they weren't smart enough to marry a chartered accountant instead) seize the moment to get all sorts of dirty jobs done.

A writer in irons will do anything to get away from the sight of the loathsome "qwertyuiop" at the top of the typewriter keyboard. Anything. Sift the kitty litter, clean the fireplace, have the dog put down, take a message to Garcia.

Blockage strikes at any time out of the blue. One day you rattle off Mr. Editor's 1,500 words with one hand while trimming the kiddies' hair with the other. Next day you're seized up tighter than the St. Lawrence in January.

I've come across only one book on the subject, a bunch of pseudo-scientific claptrap entitled *Right Brain, Write On*. The premise is that if you can somehow shut off the left side of your brain, then the right side — where all the "creativity" is supposed to be bottled up — cuts in and your blockage gives way with a mighty floosh.

I couldn't master the knack. Trying to put the left side on hold with a brick was worse than useless. Paralyzing the whole cranium with a quart of gin surpassed the brick in inffec ... ineffish ... inefficaciousness.

What the book did give me was the cold comfort that I am not alone. All the biggies — Mailer, Steinbeck, Hemingway, Pinter, et al. — testified that they often suffered the terrible pangs of writer's block. And I imagine that being seized up solid with a publisher's advance of $3 million dangling just out of reach must be quite like the far side of hell.

What was different about the biggies was that the great majority of them claimed to have been successful in dynamiting their mental log jams with hootch. That may be so considering the large number of them who've snuffed it as raging dipsos. But in this particular, I have found no release in the bottle.

Oh, the fingers finally slip into gear, no doubt, but the result is gibberish twice as convoluted as when one is not chemically enhanced.

Maybe the difference is that when you're in the 45-per-word bracket even claptrap is considered the creation of genius. On the other hand, probably not. I think what I just spat out was a sour grape.

Others among the big-time boys said they beat their blocks by sitting them out. Suddenly, they claimed, they slipped into some sort of creative trance and produced page after page, not conscious at the end of having done it.

I've tried that, too. No go. It alarms the missus and puzzles the children — "Mummy, why has daddy been staring at the wall since last July with nearly all his hair pulled out?"

It's like trying to force yourself to go to sleep. As the midnight minutes tick by the rigidity of your whole person increases, the nerves become taut as harp strings, until you're wider awake than a favourite nephew at the reading of the Last Will and Testament.

Plagiarism is the only way I've found to bust a block but that can be used only a few times per annum. Most scriveners plagiarize, I'm sure — themselves, I mean. Stephen Leacock claims he sold even his laundry list at least five times.

I've tried other methods but they'd never slip past even a 40-watt editor. Short paragraphs is one.

Like this.

You take the one pitiful little idea you have.

And stretch it out.

Thus.

It's a desperate ploy to get to the end of the last page with your gas gauge banging against "empty."

I do have one incident of real plagiarism on my conscience. Once, at a newspaper, I parroted a rival columnist word for word except for saying "should" where he said "should not" and the other way around.

The trauma was so great I never tried that prank again. Not a soul noticed! Not the editors, not the readers, not even the other columnist. I sobbed bitterly as my high notions of tens of thousands of constant and alert readers went up in a blue flash.

I've pooped out on prayer, too: "Dear Lord, haven't I been a good little lad for weeks, chucking fistfuls of change to poor winos, holding doors for pensioners, suffering City Fathers to live ... not quite Mother Teresa but close. If ever I meet a leper on Water Street ...

"Lord, may I cash in a rain check? How about a tailor-made comical occurrence just outside the window? Let's say a priest and a rabbi and a Protestant clergyman just happen to be driving past and ... I leave it to you. Nothing too elaborate, just something I can squeeze 1,500 words from." But what do my pious supplications get me? "Return to Sender," that's what.

Living with a blocked writer must be rather like having a cross between a homicidal maniac and a short-circuited robot on the premises. The cats scramble for the high ground, the children are whimpering under the bed, the screams of anguish and despair bring round the constables.

Slumping for hours, glazed-eyed and twitching or roaring back and forth the house laying down horrendous curses on the day and the hour you ever decided to take up such a crucifying trade.

It isn't pretty. And now that many writers have got expensive computers the economic toll in the profession will be monstrous. Because at least once in a twelvemonth there comes to each of us the savage urge to turn upon the tools of the wretched trade and pulverize them.

Well, luckily, I had no great seizure with this month's effort. It all went tickety-boo, no blockage, no congestion — maybe that new "Fruit'n'Fibre" had something to do with it.

I mean, you've never read this piece before. Have you?

HI-JINKS IN A TOURIST
MECCA

Newfoundland is getting its fair share of the 27 tourists who did *not* go to Expo '86 this year.

So welcome to the Happy Province, Mr. and Mrs. Dwayne Spritzer of Des Moines! Sorry you took a wrong right turn at the border but now that you're here we'll try to be extra nice to you. The only "Scream Machine" we have is the House of Assembly and, unfortunately, that's closed for the summer.

But there are myriad other attractions. Having your snap taken next to the Come by Chance road sign is a great thrill for some, although admittedly, not quite on a par with La Scala. A pity you didn't get here before "Famish Gut" transubstantiated itself into "Fair Haven."

You have but to add a mere 400 miles to your route, though, to collect a relatively new one ... the town of Sheshatshit on the shores of Grand Lake in Labrador. It means, in the language of the native people, "the place where the river meets the lake." The official CBC pronunciation is, approximately, "Shesh-a-shee," but that lot usually errs on the side of prudence.

While you're there you might as well compensate yourself for not having seen the treasures of the Pharaohs by a side jaunt to Tumble Down Dick Island on the Labrador Coast.

It's named for Oliver Cromwell's son, Richard, who was an epileptic and was nicknamed, in those heartless days before Ed Broadbent, "Tumble Down Dick."

Some tourists are greatly disappointed that not all Newfoundlanders spend their spare time knocking cute little baby seals on the conk. They expect we do it like Rambo thrashing a full division of Russkis. But I, myself, a typically colourful and quaint native (photos, $9.98 next to your lady wife) could not stay in the same house where seal meat was being cooked.

I was traumatized in youth. I struck a tin of seal that had gone off, and in mid-January was confined to the outhouse for three days running. Isn't that an interesting little tidbit for your Newfoundland book of memories!

Yes, the Canadian pavilion at Expo isn't everything. It's too bad you couldn't get here for our world-famed Dandelion Festival. People gasp in awe and astonishment at this natural spectacle and exclaim,"Oh, look, there's another one, very like the first." Some are stewed and eaten but the vast majority are not. Life's funny.

A curious fact that might interest you is that according to a federal study done in 1978, it takes people in smaller towns like Port aux Basques 9.3 seconds longer to walk 50 feet than it does people in larger towns like St. John's.

But it's more likely our natural wonders that will seize your attention. Not for you those garish displays of Mayan art and floating restaurants at Expo. One of our biggest draws in the natural line here is fog.

Ours is not the effete, piffling sort which, as the poet tells us, "creeps in on little cat feet." Ours is the dense, robust sort of fog and is sometimes compared, by those who've seen them both, to elephant patties. Some spots are more favoured than others — Port aux Basques hasn't been seen in nearly three years and neither has the survey team sent out to look for it.

Imagine the excited chatter at your next cocktail party in swinging Des Moines when you bring out your souvenir tin of genuine Newfoundland fog ... produced by an outfit in New Brunswick! By the way, if you've ever been to Taiwan you'll notice that their souvenirs are stamped "Made in Newfoundland."

Then there's the human side which can make or break any vacation. We in Newfoundland are kind, hospitable, charming, helpful, considerate, fascinating, witty, colourful, quaint and just plain, gosh-darn nice. I've already mentioned myself in this connection but rest assured there are tens more like me as my "Take a quaint, charming, etc. native to lunch," display at the airport explains.

(En passant, I might mention that I have managed to procure a quantity of Expo '86 postcards and for a modest consideration you may avoid the jeers and degradation of the folks back home if they find out you ended up in St. John's instead of Vancouver.)

Then, of course, there are the many fêtes, festivals and fairs, the largest, the most boisterous and far-famed of which is the annual Provincial Vacuity Festival held at St. John's the first fog-free Monday in August, or on Labour Day, whichever comes first.

This event is what Newfoundland's all about and has been celebrated here since time out of memory. In the final contest of the day all the winners of the previous heats compete for the most vacuous Newfoundland crown. As twilight gathers on the shores of old Quidi Vidi Lake the crackling excitement in the air is almost palpable.

The finalists sit around with their chins in their hands sighing desperately and try to out-vacuate each other, e.g., "She's gone, byes, she's gone." "Eeyep, she's really gone, bye, absolutely, utterly and completely gone." The judge's job is not an easy one.

Another spectacle you won't see in Des Moines (and certainly not at your boring old Expo) are the In Memoriam notices in the local newspaper. This custom is said to have originated in Ireland soon after movable type was invented. Long departed dear ones are saluted by poetical tributes selected from the paper's mid-Victorian catalogue. Don't be too hasty in saying that reading In Memoriam notices seems to lack a certain intellectual adventurousness until you've read the rest of the paper.

In the unlikely event that you have a few spare moments why not, ah well, ah, you know, why not ... drive to Come by Chance again and take some more snaps in front of the road sign. Can't be too careful with those film-eating airport x-rays. In Come by Chance it takes them nearly four minutes to walk 50 feet and the undertakers have made not a few tragic mistakes.

Of course, if a mad round of frantic excitement and thrills is not your cup of tea we have the more tranquil pursuits like sitting in your car in the ferry lineup or waiting for the restaurant to re-open after lunch or perhaps just relaxing for a few days outside some quaint, colourful garage while they change your muffler. Come share our lukewarmth.

Naturally, the great magnet of your visit will be the capital city of St. John's. Here, the premier cultural attraction is hanging around the shopping malls. Be warned, though, that chucking loose change into the indoor fountains is not for the faint of heart!

Yes, Mr. and Mrs. Dwayne Spritzer of Des Moines, please rest assured that you, as Newfoundland's tourist industry for 1986, can expect a hearty welcome, an exciting sojourn and a long farewell.

P.S. If there's nobody home the key is under the mat.

COMPUTER ENVY HITS COLUMNIZERS

It's envy, impure and simple, which prompts me to note that some of my fellow columnizers have got hold of computers.

Wish I had one. I fancy that a computer would make the wretched task of writing a column deliriously easy. The rag bag of the human mind has got a limited number of bits and pieces in it whereas a computer has got a host of rag bags all chucked together and on electronic tap.

As time passes, the craft of computerized columnization will become more refined. It will be harder to tell them from the hand-whittled sort. But right now, the joints show.

An example of a column done by computer: "Speaking of cabbages, the largest cabbage ever reared was grown by Lubianka Zinkoski in what was then Upper Silesia in 1946. It weighed 176 (or whatever) kilograms.

"World cabbage production hit an all-time high in 1984 when enough of the vegetable was harvested to fill 7.43 million box cars.

"The average Australian family eats 16.8 heads of cabbage per year whereas in Patagonia ... " But enough of cabbage, surely. You get the general drift of computerized columnization. A button is pushed, a subject is designated and the "retrieval system" goes to work like 10,000 devils on double pay spewing out everything the human race knows of cabbage including the number of cheap boarding houses on the globe that reek of Jeye's Fluid and boiled wassaname.

The envy I have of computer-users is not untinged by fear, the fear of being left behind in the dust. Once they get the wrinkles ironed out, you may not be able to tell a hand-crafted column from a computerized one. I figure I've got five years left at best.

That's why my day is made when the bank computer tells me my overdraft equals the national debt of Argentina or when the person at the supermarket checkout computer goes berserk and pounds her machine with both fists screaming, "Abort launch! Abort launch!"

I jump for joy whenever I read in a newspaper that "A spokesman for the department of enough cabbages were harvested in 1984 to fill 7.43 million boxcars declined comment." I rejoice because I know the mysterious sentence was written by a newsperson sitting at a computer terminal ... a terminal not yet quite capable of terminating its operator.

Computerphobia is, I'm comforted to learn, a widespread thing. Many of us were traumatized a few years back when the news magazines assured us that without a knowledge of computers we were like a basket of kittens in the middle of a highway with a steam-roller bearing down. We would be the new illiterates.

I realized I wasn't alone in this condition when David Suzuki came to town — knowing all that may possibly be known about fruit flies and computers — and denounced the seal hunt.

A letter to a St. John's newspaper said, "Dear Sir, Does that fellow call himself David Christ or is he Jesus Suzuki?" It wasn't the seal hunt that set the correspondent off, I think, as much as it was the intimidating presence of so overwhelming a fruit fly computer expert. I have since met many such computerphobes.

My apprehension leaps whenever I read a piece by Nova Scotia writer, Silver Donald Cameron. I didn't notice any joints whatsoever in his stuff. Yet, a few years ago, Silver Donald was kind enough to send me details of his home computer system at a time when I thought I'd better get computerized or go under.

It was then my ambition to retire to a rural area, toss off push-button columns in the blink of an eye and devote the rest of my time to increasing the world's production of cabbages.

Professor Cameron has, by now, either mastered the computer perfectly so as to produce articles without seam or he tired of the apparatus early on and pitched it off the D'Escousse government wharf.

"Information retrieval systems" are what the hellish devices are sometimes called. "User-friendly" is the odd phrase their makers use to describe them. I get a nervous bowel whenever I see the Charlie Chaplin lookalike demolish a mountain of paperwork in seconds because I'm reminded that there's nothing between me and extinction but a 1968 "Royal" manual with a quarter pound of cigarette ash in its works.

I dread the doorbell. Two chances out of three, it's a couple of the rising generation wanting you to sponsor them in a walk-run-bike-rock-dance or spit-a-thon so they can buy ... what else? ... a computer for their school. It's another twist of the mid-life crisis blade for a computerphobe has-been like me.

Therapy has been of little help. I gave it up after the first half-dozen sessions. The most Dr. Kiniski could offer was that since journalism consists largely of telling lies and that since a liar with a poor memory is the most pitiable specimen of humanity imaginable, therefore I resent and dread the computer's super-memory.

I have met several minor novelists who have the same problem. They're marooned in the age of the goose quill while most of their contemporaries have taken the leap into the Valley of the Silicon. Computerized novelists have sales in the millions but here, too, the butts still show.

Every now and then the electronics flicker, and dab in the middle of a trashy novel you may get, "Jessica knew that the sadistic neo-Nazi who possessed the formula to destroy the world's supply of cabbages was only minutes behind her as she scrambled desperately across the Finnish tundra/the wastes of Patagonia/the cruel burning sandstone of the Nularbor Plain."

It was my silly conservatism that lost me the computer race and left me on the scrap-heap of columnization. It was pigheadedness. If someone tells me I must, must, must see "Seed Catalogues: Part II, the Movie" I make it a point never to do so.

It was the same when, in the early days of "word processors," the things were urged upon me. I pooh-poohed them. "Word processors," I spat scornfully, "Might as well stick your Funk and Wagnalls into the Cuisinart with balsamic vinegar and fling the results against the wall!"

But who's laughing now? Not me with my fingertips bloody, crumpled typewriter paper ankle-deep, persecuted by deadline-crazed editors, the crucial entry in my Webster's obscured by the kiddies' Crayolas, shouting rude words at Jehovah's Witnesses, making improper gestures at enlightened juveniles collecting for a school computer ...

No, it certainly isn't a jolly Friar Guy hunched over his manuscript in the guttering light of a candle cringing under the cruel lash of the Brother Superior which falls upon his stooped shoulders at each and every blot.

THE DEVIL AND HIS RAILWAY

S ome country, Canada. At one end of it — at Expo '86 — they're spending billions to glorify transportation in general and the railway in particular. At the Newfoundland end of the stick, the unsanitary end, Canadian National threatens for the umpteenth time to rip the rails up altogether.

"Hard as the devil's head," is a Newfoundland expression. It means stubborn, obstinate, pig-headed in the extreme. Possibly the only thing harder than Old Nick's noggin is Canadian National.

Newfs, en masse, have often worked themselves into a roaring blue-faced fury over CN. Turning blue isn't a pretty sight but in the world at large it sometimes gets results. It has been known to shift immovable objects in both St. John's and Ottawa.

But nothing has ever budged CN a measly millimetre. The local press club used to hold a service of remembrance of the latest of its number to abandon hope and become the railway's public relations flack.

More than one of our federal MPs has made a life's career of trying to butt CN. Possibly nothing except the seal hunt debacle caused such sustained agitation. Nothing has ever dented the devil's head.

It's uncanny, as if "The Railway" was not susceptible to any known earthly force. It has appeared to do exactly as it pleases ... 100 years after the phrase "the public be damned" fell out of favour in most of North America.

It was nearly 20 years ago that I rode the last passenger train across the island and back. "Come on with the buses!" wrote the callow youth. I was threatened with more than one knuckle sandwich on that account but by that time passenger service had become so bad that crawling to Port aux Basques on your hands and knees wasn't much worse.

Train-savers argue to this day that it was deliberate CN policy to make train travel such a miserable experience that passengers would dwindle and they'd have an excuse to close shop. CN puts it the other way. It says that when the trans-island highway was finally paved in 1965 we all took to the horseless carriage.

In other parts of Canada the railway is elevated to mystic heights. It "saved" British Columbia, it opened the west, it bound a nation together. Just singing, filming and writing about the great Canadian railway is a small industry in itself. The New-foundland railway is just as firmly imbedded in our history and mythology. But like much else in these parts it had its own doom built into it from the start. In the words of a colonial governor: it "shall not be what is deemed in the United Kingdom or America, a firstclass railway."

This too-good-for-the-likes-of-them attitude is sometimes suspected to be alive and well and living in Ottawa. Ours was a dinky little narrow-gauge train. It could hardly go faster than a moose trot, it blew off the rails in a high wind, it got stuck in snowdrifts for weeks on end and the old passenger cars were finally shipped off to tootle through the banana groves of Honduras.

Bob Hope, Linda Darnell and half a dozen other Hollywoodites are variouly credited with calling it "The Newfie Bullet" while on entertainment tours during the Second World War. Unnamed is the distraught U.S. serviceman who heard the Bullet up around the bend, threw himself across the track and starved to death before she reached him. Or the woman who went into labour and was chided by the conductor for boarding "in that condition" and told him that at the start of the journey she hadn't been pregnant.

I once spoke to an old man who remembered Robert Reid, the one-eyed Scot who was our van Horne. To shame a wary train crew into crossing a new and fragile-looking trestle, Reid lay down under it, hands behind his head, and pretended to snore loudly.

In recent years, a descendant, Ian Reid, offered to sell back the huge right-of-way (nearly one-tenth of the island) that Robert had been given as part payment for his labours. His asking price included $1.50 for each estimated rabbit on the premises.

One of the few kind things ever said about the Bullet is that she had one of the best restaurants anywhere. The cutlery was sterling, the napery linen and the salmon a glory. But, before the fall, tinned peas and congealed pork chops were the dismal order.

In the last quarter of the 1880s, a sort of railway mania struck. Branch lines were planned and some built even to places innocent of a horse. Some cried caution but a forebear of John Crosbie, with a few nice contracts in the bag himself, roared in the legislature that, "The voice of the people is the will of God!"

One of Joey Smallwood's early achievements was to walk the 500 miles of the Newfoundland railway to start a union, collecting 50 cents in dues from each recruit. Some unkind persons still claim that he could not have otherwise afforded to get married. Another damnable lie, I'm sure.

Where I grew up, the evening's recreation was to walk three miles to the station to see the train. A few times a week there'd be passengers get on or off. If we knew this we'd put on a brisker step and one of our number would say, "Let's get in there early to hark at them roarin' and bawlin', what?"

There didn't seem to be much difference in arrivals or departures. Folks in those days took their travel seriously. They grappled and hugged one another and wept and wailed in high Victorian fashion.

They might be going or coming 50 miles or 5,000, for five days or forever but these outbursts of grief or joy seemed as gloriously soppy to us adolescent louts as *The Death of Little Nell*.

Of course, the railway did take tens of thousands of Newfoundlanders away forever and, after many long years, brought some of us back. In 1963, I sat in a day coach from Toronto to home for a fare of, if memory serves, $28.50. It was a bargain however you cut it.

That jostling, doddering tinker toy of a Bullet was the unlikely object of heavy sentiment, almost a tribal memory. Her demise stirred much of the population to a blind fury. Objectivity had nothing to do with it.

Passenger service ended nearly 20 years ago. Today's deal is said to be that if CN is allowed to rip up its rails for good, Ottawa will give us $1 billion to upgrade the highway.

Eight years ago, Frank Moores, then premier, termed any such tradeoff blackmail. Some say young Alfie has a similar attitude. With an eye to the past, I would never bet against CN.

Another piece of the Rock'll be butted and shattered by the devil's head.

PERILS OF THE FUNNY TRADE: A WORD OF CAUTION TO THE YOUNG

Good morning and thanks for inviting me along during Careers Week to Bung Hole Tickle High to speak on the topic of Journalism.

The main thing about Journalism is to eschew the funny idea of it. Once a journalist has been certified funny, his life becomes a little hell. A "funny" Journalist works twice as hard and is paid half as much.

Cracking wise puts much more strain on you than, let us say, the writing of an editorial on Pakistan or a news story on the excellent job the Board of Trade continues to do.

Journalists who have been certified funny show their age much sooner than Journalists who broadcast live from Pakistan or who actually live next door to the president of the Board of Trade.

That is a general rule in Journalism. The more serious and sober a Journalist you are the more happy and healthy a Journalist you will be.

I have known Editorial Writers (and there's no one more serious unless it's the person who has to decide between raspberry vinegar and Creole shrimp in the "lifestyle" section) ... I have known Editorial Writers who once wrote seriously that Mr. Hitler was a man to be watched.

They have gloomed merrily along and today are writing seriously that Mr. Gorbachev is a man to be watched — and they're still bright as buttons and play a hard game of squash.

On the other hand, a Journalistic "humourist" is a pitiful sight. He slopes around town in a grubby raincoat with a flask of cheap rye in the pocket, spitting into a dirty handkerchief. He was certified funny only a few short years ago and has since humoured himself into a slushy puddle.

Ah, yes, students of Bung Hole Tickle High. I know. I stand here today as living proof of the perils of being a "funny" Journalist. Here to warn you, here to entreat you, here to beg you to be a serious Journalist, to train for the "lifestyle" section of the newspapers or programs like *Midday* on the CBC.

You'll live to see your children grow up and become dentists, your BMW dealer ask you to join his bridge club and the still-young-and-glamourous widow of some Journalistic "humour" writer ask you for advice about the carpet for her new apartment.

How does it all start? We must go back to the Caesars of ancient Rome. They were sort of like modern-day mayors of Halifax except they kept lions.

Away would go Caesar to the wars. Away to loot Truro, to despoil Sydney, to lay Lunenburg bare to the foxes and crows. And home would come Caesar in triumph, laden with spoils and trophies, home across the MacDonald Bridge as the citizens of Halifax cheered him to the skies.

But do you know, students of Bung Hole Tickle High, that whispering in great Caesar's earhole at his very moment of triumph was an early model of the Journalistic wisecracker?

"It won't last, Julie baby," he would say. "Even you will one day snuff it. Here, have another humble pill."

And to the crowds this official joker would shout: "Hail, Caesar? Don't make me laugh, already. Loot Truro? Ha, this turkey couldn't tear the skin off a rice pudding. Listen, people. Caesar is ugly, ugly, ugly and his mother dresses him funny."

Being a joker back in those days wasn't easy. If he went too far he was fed to the imperial lions. It was a nervewracking job and he grew old, if at all, long before his time.

Not so the Editorial Writer who chipped out editorials in the Rome Gazette along the lines of "Julie Does it Yet Again" or the editor of the "lifestyles" section who wrote that the Forum should be redone in purple. They went on to quadro chariots and second villas out in Chester.

Today, of course, the official jester doesn't have to fear offending the mayor of Halifax although I warn you, prospective Journalists, to step lightly with His Worship of St. John's.

And so, history marched on. The Celts, the Jews, King Lear, Old King Cole — they all had official jesters. In Newfoundland right down to the present century nearly every community had its fool and he was called "the wonderful quare hand."

He stood on his head, capered about, clicked his heels and spouted amusing gibberish. His job was to make public mock of the merchant, the priest and the constable so as to make the people believe they weren't absolutely helpless.

The quare hand could sometimes even shame the community triumvirate into a modicum of humility or make the people giggle so hard that they dropped their rocks and clubs. But pay was low and the poor fool often ended up in the poor house or the lunatic asylum at an early age.

Then came Modern Journalism and the lot of an official fool improved immensely. Which isn't saying much. The imperial lions were no more and mayors west of St. John's were generally enlightened — but raw nerves and an early pauper's grave still loom large.

At cocktail parties and other such pornographic functions he is often pounced upon by strangers who say, "Why Mr. Yug, so you're the funny man, ha, ha, ha."

And Yug replies, "cold weather we're having, isn't it?" at which the stranger rolls around the floor laughing fit to bust a gut.

So Yug, perplexed, adds, "but I hear it may warm up tomorrow," at which the stranger stares rudely then stomps off in a huff glaring back at the biggest, damndest unfunny fraud that ever was.

Editors laugh long and loud at poor certified-funny Yug — but only when he offers to write them a "serious" piece. Producers have been known to giggle themselves into a hernia over Yug, but only if he submits a commentary on Pakistan.

"Crack wise, crack wise," they say. "My six-year-old kid has got a million of 'em. Here's one for free if you promise to use it."

And so it is, students of Bung Hole Tickle High, that I entreat you by both personal and historical example to steer well clear of Funny Journalism. Set your sights on the serious branches of the profession such as sports or social notes. Get yourself certified serious soon after you step inside a newsroom door.

That way lies fame, fortune, respect, the Canada medal, a seat in the Senate and — for those who reach the very top of the serious Journalistic ladder — a chain of chicken takeaways located right across the street from high schools like this.

And so, dear students, as you ponder your futures now during Careers Week a few will say: "Is Journalism for me?"

Old Yug can only answer: "Journalism? Be Serious!"

ADVENTURES OF A NEWFOUNDLAND WRITER IN DARKEST MAINLAND

Nobody has actually seen Port aux Basques for the past 50 years or so. We must take it as an article of faith it's there somewhere in deep fog. In August, while standing in line at the CN ferry, I bent down to get a pebble out of my shoe and found myself fumbling with someone else's ankle. "Hoy! What's going on down there?" came a baritone from above. "You one of them drug crazed hippies or what?"

I apologized to the unseen gent and his obscured ankle but was grateful that he kept muttering about the present generation and the blame resting squarely on the parents because it was only by sound alone that you could navigate through that profound murk and keep place in the queue.

On the ferry there was an ancient mariner, a retired doryman from the south coast, who was insatiable in his pursuit of someone to yarn with ... or at. The old fellow's technique was to lean on the rail, wait for an approaching victim and stop him in his tracks by spurting tobacco juice on the deck a foot in front of the person's toes.

Then, without a how-de-do, he'd launch into it: "I minds the time we were crossin' here — in 19 and 52 — no, I tell a lie — in 19 and 53 and she struck a whale. Stark, calm, no fog. Well, sir, the captain ... "

Most Canadians paused briefly, stared at him for a looney old geezer, then continued onward at a much brisker pace. But he finally gaffed something of a kindred soul in the person of a retired Jewish doctor from San Francisco.

The pair nattered away for nearly an hour, mostly on marine topics. The doryman told the doctor that what you must do when you see an extra big wave bearing down on your dory is to pick up a little fish about so long and pitch it over the head of her into the wave. This gesture, without fail, caused the wave to flatten out without damage to life or property.

Well, hell, now wasn't that a coincidence. Because last year while cruising the Mediterranean the doctor had noted the same custom among Greek fishermen, a small world the nautical one.

Trees make the difference on the Mainland. There's said to be a slight family resemblance between bits of the Maritimes and bits of Newfoundland but, generally, it's chalk and cheese. In Newfoundland you have spruce and bog, bog and spruce with a sprinkling of birch throughout.

But once across the Gulf you get oak, maple, aspen and pine growing in places out of soil that, as someone said about the American corn belt, "looks good enough to eat without first passing it through vegetables." At a leak-gas-ice cream stop in the middle of New Brunswick, a fellow countryman spotting the licence plates walked over to me and said: "Ah, boy, this is some sweet country they got here, innit?"

Exactly so, brother, exactly so. They talk queer, too, don't they? A common request when one is abroad is to "say something in the Newfie accent." Well, which one do you want, there are probably dozens.

Lots in the Maritimes, too, I expect, but the casual transient can distinguish only a few. It's a bit squealy and lispy in Cape Breton, as when the singer, John Allen Cameron, pipes up from the stage, "Are you with me, people?" In northern Nova Scotia folks sound clipped, a bit nasal and a trifle dry while in the middle of New Brunswick it is more of a soft drawl, quite pleasant to listen to.

Newfoundlanders are foolish drivers and you can count on at least one brush with death every 20 miles. The one fault with Maritime motorists is that they sniff each other's tails like a conga line of dogs in heat. It's curious to see, on a highway that's dead straight for miles, 10 or 15 vehicles hurtling along with a hair's breadth between them.

It is astonishing to reflect, in parts of New Brunswick, that the piece of tortuous country lane you're driving on is the main road linking one part of the nation of Canada to the other. God willed it that way, I suppose, rather than political patronage entering into it. On that point we're strictly virginal here in the Happy Province and so can't judge.

For the first half-hour or so the carnage along the Maritime roads is a shock. Then you get used to it. The squashed and bloody corpses of raccoons, skunks and porcupines are unknown on Newfoundland island because there are no live ones to start with.

Or snakes, or rabbits, or deer, or cougars, or coyotes or half the variety of field and forest birds, or, until lately, squirrels. Exotic woods teeming with exotic wildlife ... it all seems almost tropical in the interior Maritimes. Add a dash of continental heat, skies wiped clear of maritime mist and then some crashing inland thunderstorms and you've got something refreshingly different as far as a Newfoundlander is concerned.

My favourite spot was an old concrete jetty on Grand Lake, N.B., at Scotchtown at twilight. At that time of day the water, the sky, the very air turned to luminous streaks of light blue and soft pink, oddly resembling day's end in Florida. But instead of the deep, growling undertow of the ocean there was the choppy slap of the lakeshore.

On the lake, loons struck evensong, frogs or crickets began their shimmering hum in the pine and trembling aspen, and at a farm across the road a bull began to roar out of lust, hunger or contentment. Swallows darted over the molten water through dancing spirals of gnats and a distant pickup truck whispered past bound, perhaps, for beer or Baptist brimstone.

It was indeed some sweet country they had here. On the surface of it, anyway, and to the vacationer for a few weeks of summer. Possibly the winters are just as crucifying and politics, commerce and society every bit as medieval in New Brunswick as they are in Newfoundland.

Yet there are interesting differences. To us, Maritimers seem reticent to the point of being frostily tongue-tied. Some years ago, a CBC reporter moved from St. John's to Halifax and, first morning on the job, asked the boss directions to the washroom. He said he was busy but could grant her an interview in his office at 3:30 that afternoon ... you see what I mean?

For all that, the service is better and the professional welcome warmer in restaurants and motels. There's a broader cultural mix with Acadians, natives, Loyalists and others. That can be a mixed blessing.

The Acadians can be more-persecuted-than-thou, the Loyalists put on insufferable airs because their pappies once picked a barmy king over a president with wooden teeth and the natives may demand microwave ovens and unlimited salmon, too. But N.B. be thanked for marvellous holidays.

On the way back home, the ferry suddenly burst through the fog at the approaches to Placentia town. Right on cue, a returning countryman popped out on deck and whooped: "Aye, look! Be the lord liftin' Jaysus! There she is, boys! There she is!"

That, too, was the appropriate comment, for the word "sweet" cannot be easily applied to the savagely triumphant shores of Newfoundland.

FOND REMEMBRANCES OF NEWSROOMS PAST

When they were still called copy boys even a mere reporter could order them to do anything within the realm of good taste — fetch coffee, pop around the corner for a flask, run out and cash cheques.

They were young, spotty lads, miserably paid but keen as mustard to be part of the great newspaper world. Last I heard, their title had been changed to that of "communication clerks" after which they put on airs and would neither lead nor drive.

We once had a chappie who lasted only a week. He was a merry and mischievous lad much given to playing pranks. One day one of the paper's top management, a large man subject to a weak heart, was leaning over a stair rail to answer the phone. Our Puck came round a corner, saw this fine target and goosed it ferociously while letting out a screech like a banshee.

He was let off with a caution, but only a few days later he heard footsteps coming down the corridor and hid behind some filing cabinets. Then he hurled himself out into the path, his hands up like talons and shouted, *"RAAaaaarrr!"* Again it was the boss with the dicey ticker.

One more chance he was given and one more chance he took. It was Saturday morning and the cardiac-arrest candidate was seated at the city desk, reading a paper. Our hero came out of his cubicle, saw there was someone behind the newspaper and crawled stealthily under the desk.

Then he sharply grabbed an ankle and growled savagely like a German shepherd — another of his favourite tricks. He was let go without references.

Sports reporters are notoriously callous. Ours soon discovered that a new copy boy was terrified of the dark. They would quietly position themselves around the newsroom and slam out all the lights at once. He would dive under a desk and wouldn't come out until the sun came up the next day.

Meanwhile, the wire copy machines, his responsibilty, continued to spew forth paper and tape all through the night and by dawn the chaos was incredible. More merciful souls offered to take up a collection so's he could seek help but he refused. Doctors were another one of his many phobias.

Another lad made a practice of dumping wastebaskets full of water on his colleagues as they came out the door three storeys below. One day, he tipped ten gallons toward his pal going out but struck the president of the Chamber of Commerce coming in. Of course, odd behaviour wasn't confined to the copy boys. Before my time (so this is hearsay) a certain reporter was subject to fits of depression. Whenever the glooms came over him, his ambition was to get out a window, swing hand over hand to the middle of the streeet on the telephone cable and drop down in front of a passing municipal bus.

The Canadian Press correspondent of the time was assigned to keep an eye on the moody one, to seize him around the legs if he went for the window and to bawl for help. As an extra precaution, or in case of laryngitis, he always wore a referee whistle.

Nut case was let go when, while doing an article on nightlife in St. John's, he was discovered by the editor in the middle of the news desk doing hands-on research with the city's most notorious tart. Needless to say he has since gained a high position in politics.

Harold Horwood and Farley Mowat, both good sports so names may be named, once came into the newsroom in the wee hours in an exhilarated but socialist-minded condition — if such a thing is possible.

They were aghast at the battered wrecks of typewriters the workers were forced to toil over so they pitched them all out the window to the sidewalk below. Much good that did the downtrodden proletariat. Management had the machines collected, hammered back into some sort of shape and capitalism as we know it rolled on.

With tools and manpower of this calibre it was little wonder the sheet was often riddled with mistakes. At the peak of the ecumenical movement there was a picture on the front page of some local clergy smirking hypocritically at one another. "Protestants and Christians hold meet," said the cutline.

Or how about, "Poverty committee reports; hundreds in city reduced to tarpaper snacks." The competition was, if anything, even worse. On the morning following the death of a local society matron two of their headlines were butted together: Ann Landers Says Sex IS Possible after Sixty, and Mrs. X Dies After Second Stroke.

Of course, there were some moments of inspiration. Joey Smallwood, then on the skids, led off the dance at a Liberal bash with a lithesome young chickee who wore a backless evening dress. The picture was headlined, The Naked and the Dead.

There used to be a bloody great Russian and his missus doing the circuits performing feats of strength — towing strings of locomotives from a standing start, playing catch with Volkswagons and so forth. I did a feature article on them.

"The portion of the crowd standing downwind of them had to be taken off and given oxygen ... He looked like a cross between Rasputin and King Kong ... The female of the species tended to break wind when she really put her back into it and there were fears that this might touch off the Civil Defence sirens," were some of the phrases.

Next day, the newsroom had just settled back into harness after lunch when the elevator commenced to groan and shudder, and when those two hairy mammoths sidled out of it all hands hit the deck in a body.

Ivan the Terrible started to pound the desk with a hand the size of a pig's backside. Finally, a sports reporter with the nickname of Pee-Wee because of his short stature was pushed forward. He had one arm in a cast already so we figured he had one less bone to break.

"Iss vary good article in your paper, yes," roared the Bolshi Bunyan. "Could we have copies for frans, pliss?"

Every living soul on the premises scuttled forward with an armload of papers and the fragrant couple punished the elevator down to ground level again. It wasn't their fault that the bathtub was never made that would fit them.

A great peril for reporters was having to take death notices over the phone. Because the grieving survivors were in such a stressful situation, they could be as touchy as hornets over the slightest mistake or misprint. A large and bloodthirsty family came roaring once when it was reported that their dear wife and mother had "Pissed peacefully away at St. Clare's Mercy Hospital ... "

We used to call the proofreading office the CNIB but it served a useful purpose because you could generally shift the blame for your own mistakes to that direction.

Politicians use the civil service to the same good advantage so it is small wonder that so many journalists, ready-trained, bolt the ranks and go over to join the rats.

JANUARY'S AWFUL. BUT, THANK GOD, AT LEAST WE'RE SAFE FROM KILLER CROCODILES

In a few favoured spots like Yarmouth, N.S. or St. Andrews N.B., people's attention in January is, I suppose, taken up with the nutmeg harvest and preparations for litchi planting next month. But in most of the Atlantic region in the midst of January, when black spruce are cracked open to the heart by nights of ringing frost, our thoughts are always directed to the complete absence here of man-eating salt-water crocodiles. The hand of a merciful Providence has sprinkled the region with an adequate supply of editorial writers and/or opinion moulders who are guaranteed to latch on to our lack of crocs whenever the weather gets especially filthy.

This is the situation: An Arctic low sweeps down from Ungava. A howling blizzard roars in from the Great Lakes. A savage gale tears up from the south. Freezing drizzle slashes in from the North Atlantic. They all meet, shake hands, rejoice and do their things over the Atlantic provinces.

That's early June. In January, if anything, it's a bit worse. Power lines collapse like cobwebs before the broom, every highway is a Bermuda Triangle into which squadrons of snow plows disappear forever, and Anne Murray can goose that little snowbird until hell (Atlantic division) thaws — birdie is frozen solid on the runway.

Dick, the shepherd blows his nail but many of us blow our cool. Outages are definitely in. Power outages, phone outages, ferry outages, road outages, skull outages. People turn peevish, verging on the frantic. They huddle in corners thinking nasty things, like driving nails into Princess of Wales dollies, mounting pre-emptive strikes against the Salvation Army or voting NDP. Some have been caught as early as late November ripping all the little windows off their childrens' Advent calendars. By mid-January, the only smiling faces you see in Atlantic Canada outside of lunatic asylums are those of dipsomaniacs and the deeply religious.

Even the latter are not immune to January biliousness. A relative by marriage speaks of attending a funeral in the Baptist Belt of New Brunswick at which the pastor laced savagely into the sins of the congregation, singly and en masse. He then proceeded to launch a hair-raising attack on the corpse.

That's what an eight-month winter will do for you. But just when it seems that the tiny flame of civilization as we know it is about to gutter and die, the editorial writers come to the rescue. I'll bet my second-last oilwell there's one in your area. He's the guy who directs our attention to that man-eating salt-water crocodile lately subdued after a terrible rampage in Indonesia. Granted, he writes, we are enduring the deepest snow, the highest wind, the bitterest frost, the heaviest sleet and the Allanist MacEachen within living memory. BUT ... But we should count our blessings. Also our arms and legs. We, here in this blessed plot, this semi-demi, this other Tierra del Fuego, do not have to contend with jeezly big marine crocodiles as they do in the Celebes.

Reference is made to a news item in yesterday's issue. A monstrous croc had been captured near Kunandang in the Celebes and, on being cut open, was found to contain bits of a Buddhist monk, a Wesleyan missionary, a P and O liner and 26 local inhabitants. Everything but a loud-ticking alarm clock. It strikes you that had the missionary introduced the 26 local inhabitants to *Peter Pan* first crack out of the box, then they might have still been around to tackle the New Testament. But we digress.

I was once suspicious about the coincidence of every editorial writer in Atlantic Canada writing the same crocodile editorial every mid-January. It wasn't strange that they shared a common philosophy. Better to light one little candle than to curse the newsroom's coverage of the latest power outage. But the same time every year on the far side of the world upon which they could all pounce annually and hold up as a lamp unto our feet? So I have kept files.

Yes, there was. Last January it was Manokwari, New Guinea. In 1980, it was a village near Surabaya. So we may freeze to death in the dark secure in the knowledge that Atlantic editorialists do not — in this matter at least — take licence with the facts.

Their styles are reassuringly different, too. In St. John's there are two daily papers. The editorialist on one is a poetical humanist, while the chap on the other is scripturally kinky. Thus we may get one crocodile chin-lifter quoting Wordsworth — "not a single wassaname dies in vain, but to subserve another's gain" — and Sidney Smith's saying of strawberries that, doubtless, God could have made a better berry but doubtless, God didn't and might not that apply, whatever the weather, to our own dear crocodile-free island? In the other paper we could get an editorial telling us there's an obscure text in Thessalonians which clearly shows that while a Mighty Jehovah has so far kept killer crocs out of Canada, He could just as easily warm up the Grand Banks and sic them on us … if our youth doesn't stop wearing T-shirts with filthy words on them.

Meanwhile, they've both got their alligator bags packed and ready for the bolt to Florida.

SOME ADVICE FOR WOULD-BE WRITERS: STICK TO GUTTING CODFISH, MY SON

Nay, stick to your line and jigger, Jacky old cock" cried I. "and steer well away from the accursed trade!"

John, one of my distant and less gruesome relatives, accosts me from time to time and demands helpful hints on how to become a paid writer. He is dished off with his own calling, the fishery, and wants to turn his hand to the pen. For the sake of his late, sainted mother I do my damnedest to dissuade him, or so I tell him.

"Trot off and give Mother Teresa a hand with the latrines in Calcutta," I tell him, "or carry an old rugged cross to Vancouver on your back, or apply for auditor general of New Brunswick ... and leave the really nasty work to fools like me."

Poor deluded Jacky. I once made the mistake of telling him that I could type 45 words a minute in top gear and that a magazine column was usually 1200 words long. He got off his boots and stockings and calculated that I worked a good half-an-hour day.

"But it kind of runs in the family," he persisted. "What about great-uncle Jukes? Didn't granny used to tell us he was a great hand with the pen?"

"No, my son ... for the pen. He liked jail so well he was never content in the greater world. No sooner out than he'd crack the windows down at the Salvation Army Tabernacle and they'd pitch him back in HM Gaol again, happy as a bluearsed horse fly in stink."

"Yes, well, but there was second cousin Maudie, wasn't there?" says John. "Didn't she write so fine a letter to the Welfare one time that she got a spandered new house and a dozen Cheviot sheep out of it?"

"She would've gotten a lot more," I said, "if the minister of Welfare hadn't had a heart attack when the flash on Maudie's Brownie Hawkeye went off.

"No, John", I explained, "some of our crowd down through the years might have shown a filthy penchant for journalizing but they were smart — they either gave themselves up for electro-shock therapy or else switched their vote to the Liberals. A certain cure in either case. I'm the only real failure in that line and I'm paying the price on this side of the grave as I'm sure I will on the other."

But John is nothing if not wonderfully pig-headed. He claimed that I showed no outward wear and tear from so scurvy a life and didn't I always know where my next hot toddy was coming from? He supposed it was only a matter of coming up with ideas.

"Easier said than done," I said. "In the past 20 years I've come up with only five ideas, two of which weren't lewd. Try pounding the spit out of two suitable ideas for 20 years and there's nothing keeps your head from caving in except your eyeglasses."

Jacky was not convinced. Ideas were never a problem with him, he said. He got a new one just about every time he gutted a mackerel.

"Look old man," I said, "it might look easy but you don't know the half of it. There's editors. You must have hauled some stern-looking customers in over the gunwales in your time but you have never had any dealings with an editor. They're a constant crucifixion. They're like a wolverine whose mate you have bagged and pelted and they will stalk and torment you to Baffin Island and back. They all have a pathological fixation on a silly little thing called a deadline.

"Ah, my happy-go-lucky fisherperson," I sighed, stopping just short of rolling my eyes upward, "you don't know the terror of the poor winded bunny rabbit as the beagles draw ever nearer until you've overlooked a deadline. Miss one and you might as well have been caught relieving yourself in a baptismal font. It's a constant grinding strain which grievously abrades the nerves."

"Granted," says Jacky, "but there are little hardships in all trades. I mean, you're not exposed to all weathers, the price on the Boston market holds no terrors for you, and you can miss a quota without the poorhouse staring you straight in the face. Got her knocked, haven't you?"

Here was one tough customer and I knew it. This lad was bound and determined on straying from the paths of righteousness and embarking on a life of journalizing. I took another tack.

"Just answer me this, would you John," I said in as patient a tone as I could muster. "If you ever met a very large Dutchman, why would it never do at all to call him a monkey-sucker? Got you there, haven't I. It's because, my son, in times past in Holland it was the custom to give a spoon with the image of a monkey on the handle as a present at weddings, christenings and funerals. Large spoons, apparently, out of which toasts were drunk. A Dutch lush, you see John old trout, is called a monkey-sucker, and, if you addressed a large one as such you'd probably have to get a wooden shoe removed by surgical means."

He gave me a blank look. I smiled and shook my head sadly. Then I pressed home my point.

"If you ever want to journalize, God help you, then you must cram your wretched head with tens of thousands of useless bits of information like that in the hopes that they will someday be of use to you. Your social life is a shambles. Once too often you'll suddenly pop the subject of Dutch monkey suckers and ... " and here my voice broke.

"I was asked out to my last party, John, the month before Kennedy was shot, and anxious mothers call their children indoors whenever I pass by. For mercy sake, stick with the fishery, John. 'Twas the Apostles' own calling' as ... can you tell me who said that?"

"Weelll, perhaps you're right," replied the insufferable mulehead. "But surely there must be some advantages. I mean, you journalizers must have great larks teasing all those black-guarding big shots and getting them hopping mad."

"Now that is possibly the greatest fallacy of all," I countered. "That lot thrives on abuse like maggots on a dead whale. Spell their names right and although you've risen to new heights of scurrility, Christmas cards enclosing tickets to Florida are their only reaction."

"Say what you like," he said. "I'm at least going to give it a try."

Desperate cases require desperate cures. I took a notepad and pencil.

"Do you know," I asked, "what we journalizers earn, on the average, in the course of a mind-destroying, soul-obliterating, body-rotting year? I'll write it down for you. Look, my son, and save yourself alive!"

He blanched and staggered slightly. He backed quickly away. Gesturing a hasty goodbye he started to walk and broke into a brisk trot.

"Hey, Jacky," I called after him. "Where are you off to so fast? I've told you the best about this racket; don't you want to hear the darker side?"

"I'se the boy that builds the boat," he shouted back over his shoulder, "and I'se the boy that sails her ... "

It was a close call but I think I managed it quite nicely. As any journalizer will tell you, we'll go to spectacular lengths to discourage others from this trade. We do not want every Tom, Dick or Jacky horning in on this, the most splendid and wonder-ful racket in the world.

IF B.C.'S SO PERFECT, HOW COME THERE AREN'T MORE NEWFOUNDLANDERS THERE?

Gawking at mountains was one of my favourite pastimes while in British Columbia. It was a five-minute walk to a beach from the house where we stayed in Victoria and sometimes I would perambulate down in the afternoons and sit on a piece of dead tree about four feet in diameter and wait for the mountains to appear.

They are American mountains but, as I understand it, on permanent loan to that part of B.C. for gawking purposes. American but also perfidious. Sometimes they show up and sometimes they don't. It adds to their fascination.

Having been reared where there are some jeezly big hills but (apart from the Torngats in Labrador) no mountains, I like to look at some whenever I get the rare chance.

The thing about this particular batch of bumps is that they are on the other side of a small piece of Pacific Ocean and it is generally always foggy over there. Not fog, as we know fog, but a serious permanent dripping condition. If you sit there on your log long enough, the wind will veer or whatever and the fog will be smeared away and there will be your mountains ... every bit as nice as the ones they have in Bonne Bay.

But stay a bit longer. By and by, another veil will be drawn aside and there is another gigantic rank of mountains standing behind the first. Now, this is more like it ... more like the mountains you see in all those books and calendars and brochures which are printed on half the trees cut in B.C. every year to tell the rest of the world how beautiful British Columbia is.

Jolly good mountains, these. I can take the Pacific Ocean or leave it. It is ridiculously large to my taste. I'm afraid of it. The Atlantic Ocean no more scares me than would your average piss pot. I have got friends and relatives at the bottom of it which rather endears it to me and I wouldn't get up from even an indifferent supper to walk down to St. John's harbour to shake hands with the latest dear old idiot who's crossed the Atlantic Ocean astride a large popsicle stick. It is a lovely ocean. But the Pacific Ocean takes up too much room. Valuable room that might otherwise be taken up by land.

While sitting there on my log looking at this magnificent range of mountains and sort of waiting for the Pacific Ocean to go away and make better sense, there was another shift in the atmospherics across the straits in America and I blinked twice and thought to myself, "Sweet suffering lifting Jesus." Or thoughts to that effect. It was thought in as reverent a manner as I am capable of. For behind the first two ranks of mountains there appeared a third, so high up that nothing had any business being that far up above the horizon but clouds.

Mountains on calendars are one thing but coming face to face with the genuine article is another. I always used to think that making my first acquaintance with a mountain of consequence would make me feel humble and small and send me into the blue funks for the rest of my life. Quite the reverse. Quite.

Yes, I know, it is all very well for me to talk large about mountains having only been there within gawking distance of some while on holidays for the month of August but I cannot conceive of my attitude toward them changing in the slightest. If I had my way the bloody old Pacific Ocean would be at least half mountains.

Perhaps if I lived in that part of the world for any length of time I would get as foolish as the rest of them over there. British Columbians are weird, real weird. You will sometimes meet the scattered one who is almost a normal human being like ourselves but the illusion is soon shattered.

Their fatal flaw is that they are worried about having nothing at all to worry about. It would draw tears to the eyes of any upright decent Christian. Especially Newfoundland ones. They are in a constant state of anguish. Their minds are troubled, night and day. Missionaries should be sent out to save them.

"We have got a perfectly adequate set of mountains," they wail. "We have got what is definitely the biggest ocean in the world; we have got all the Albertans we want who can pay their way to get in here; we have got Allan Fotheringham and, on top of him, Alan Thicke. What, leave all this one day," they moan most piteously, "and go to a cruddy place like heaven?"

A severely troubled people is the result of all this. The very thought of there being no place in this world or the next better than British Columbia haunts them night and day. It would take a vast horde of British evangelists of the same calibre as those who turned a white man's hell like Africa into what it is today to lift British Columbia into the realm of contented civilization. God knows, I'd never attempt to tackle it singlehandedly. B.C. must look elsewhere for its Schweitzer or its Rhodes. Possibly, some help may arrive from the direction of Hong Kong.

Some former citizens of that general area did hail me as I sat on my log, mountain gawking. Spoke to me, in point of fact. Even went so far as to let me sit watch over their purses for them as they went about picking up bits of seaweed for their soup. A dozen other nationalities, including Albertans, nodded the time of day or at least left me in peace to my gawking. But in a whole month on that beach never did I see another Newfoundlander. I have been on more than one beach in my time but never one on which there was such a complete and merciful absence of my fellow countrymen. The answer to B.C.'s basic problem sprang to my mind in a flash ... much clearer, I venture to say, than John's revelations occurred to him at Patmos.

After that, I had to bite my tongue whenever face to face with yet another obviously troubled British Columbian. "Take heart," I might have said. "I have discovered a bloody great redeeming flaw here in this accursed paradisical super natural."

"Stop worrying," I could have told them. "If B.C. was so excruciatingly perfect as you dread it is, then you'd see a lot more Newfoundlanders on the beaches than you do. After all, we do have the pick of the world, you know, unlike those poor stunned New Brunswickers."

But I said nothing. That information might have cheered them up and the shock thereby might have been fatal. A whole lot of dead British Columbians with no place better to go to is the last thing in the world I want on my conscience. It is already loaded down with too many live Newfs in the same predicament.

THE PERILOUS ART OF "HUMPHING" FOR THE CAMERAS

A quick call to Cary Grant or Elwy Yost might have saved me worlds of grief. But oh no. When the chance came for me to stick my face on the public screen I sprang for it like a starving trout to the fly. I can now compare notes with Messrs. Grant and Yost about the pain of the hook.

Here's therapy, I thought. Here's joining the Toastmasters or Dale Carnegie and getting paid for it. For one so skittish about public speaking as to break out in hives from talking to his mother on the telephone, it seemed like the best cold-turkey cure for bashfulness on the horizon.

"All you'll have to do," they assured me, "is pull a few faces and say 'Humph!' on request. Oh, yes, and never glance directly at the camera when its little red light is lit." Since this is pretty much what I do around the house anyway, lit or unlit, I said what the hell. Why not? Sure thing, I'd trot along and make out to be the star boarder, Jack, on a CBC series about a fictional St. John's boarding house.

That was three or so years back. During the first year, this making of faces was a thing of exquisite agony, the second, one of affecting a pleasant boredom with the whole business and, after that, it was largely a matter of being snuck up on and kidney-punched by nasty little boys in drug stores.

In early days they had the devil's own job of it getting me to say even "Humph!" on cue. I would say, "Eh? Oh. Yes. Humph! How's that?" and there'd be agonized screeches from the chaps hunched over the Star Trekky console. I practised "humphing" during every waking hour around the house and while looking in the rear view mirror in the car. There's no better method of collecting rude gestures and coarse threats than driving around St. John's while scowling and saying "Humph!" Even a day's umbrage, thus collected, would demoralize the Ayatollah.

Waiting around to "humph" for the camera was torture. My bowels churned, my forehead perspired and quease was my constant companion.

Self-hypnosis, gin, acupuncture — nothing helped. Small wonder that some of my fellow artistes muttered about bread-snatching rank amateurs until I had to pin my ACTRA card to my lapel. It wasn't one of them, I'm sure, who told an aging relative of mine that what I was doing in there in "Sin John's" (which is how all good baymen see and pronounce it) was "humphing" in front of the camera. Poor soul, she got the impression that I was involved in a porno movie being made, for some strange reason, aboard the defunct Newfie Bullet. Before long comes a phone call from mother. But she really knew, in her heart, that I had neither the dignity nor the figure for such an undertaking.

By the second year I was well over the hump. Whole sentences and even short paragraphs held no terrors for me. Indeed, I suppose the pendulum swung violently the other way. To be frank, I took to flouncing. For one episode, Gordon Pinsent appeared at the door of our TV boarding house. I found it hard thereafter not to begin a conversation by saying, "Gordie, as we call him, was telling me the other day ... " I spoke of "my producer" and "my director" and was loud in the picking of nits from *All in the Family* and the national news ... technical stuff that escapes the laity.

"Make way, make way," one's spouse would cry in a desperate attempt to keep one humble. "Here comes the multimedia star, home for his sardine sandwiches. Lock naughty pussy down in the cellar so's she won't spoil Mr. Dressup's lunch." Even the kiddies tried to help. Whenever the program came on I'd roust them out of their cots and line them up in front of the TV like sparrows on a clothesline. But they'd fidget and whimper for a switch to Knowlton Nash or Mister Bill.

Mr. Pinsent himself told the cautionary tale of how he was once flung up against the wall of an Ottawa supermarket and ordered not to move by a fellow who then dashed off to fetch his wife. "There you are, Gert," he said. "Its him. It's him. I told you I had him." "Naaaaa," says Gert. "Naaaaa. He don't look one bit the same as he do on television." "Well, thanks anyway," said hubby as they strolled away disappointedly.

By the third year of being "on the set" as we call it, I'd lost some of this theatrical verve and dash and regained some of that Uriah Heepishness which had made me such a social success in the days before TV discovered me. But by then, juvenile delinquents had started to kidney-punch me and run. Taxi drivers talked baby talk about the merits of comic books. Restaurant waiters made loud jokes about boarding house hash.

TV lays you completely open. I've had my mug in newspapers and magazines for 15 years or so, but you can generally bribe still photographers to skew your phisog this way or that to disguise your natural beauty. I was safe even at the most rabid Smallwood rallies.

Shove your face on television once and the feline is out of the sack forever. Add to it the fact that this boarding house Jacky is not a jolly person. He kicks at dogs, says "Humph!", reads comic books and would lay a fire with Tiny Tim's crutches. The oldest child keeps asking me when I'm going to get shot like "that nasthy rotting creep on Dallath." I tell her not until daddy gets paid as much as he does. Her little face drops a kilometre.

So being an artiste does have its drawbacks. Just ask Grant, Yost, or Guy. They'll tell you there are times they wish they'd taken up broccoli farming or magazine editing.

GETTING STUNG? GOING BANKRUPT? NEVER MIND, YOU'LL SAVE ON TAXES

Months have passed since the trauma, but I'm still in cardiac overdrive. I should have recognized it for the grim omen it was when, first shot out of the box, the tax accountant kicked over the baby's potty. He'd just been ushered into my office. (That is to say, the former dining room in which I do my freelance journalizing.) It's in the same house in which I also live, breathe, have my being and tread on sharp plastic Sesame Street characters in the shower.

The functions of my business premises and my domestic apartments sometimes overlap. But that isn't a fact you want to broadcast when the tax fellow has just arrived to whittle you out some T-4 credits from your total heating bill. What happened was that my younger deduction had just commenced training and this had caused the older one to regress. Sibling rivalry. Thinks the older one: Where better to hide the chamber utensil than in daddy's sanctum right under the desk?

I look for the same qualities in a tax accountant as I hope to see in EPA pilots when the fog ceiling hovers toward the lower limits. A clear eye, a level head, a slight conscientious frown. But none of that craven yellow streak you sometimes get with other airlines just when you're trying to escape six months of climatic damnation for St. Pete's Beach. As buddy peeled off one of his Argyles, I wondered how far off stride he'd been put. He said that stale pee always made his eyes smart. That set me off on a gallop for the drug store and a quart of drops to put between his swimming optics and the fine print. Nothing must go wrong.

This year, for the first time, I had Tax Canada just where I wanted them. No debits, no credits ... I'd already contributed my full share for the fiscal year.

There were only the paper formalities but still, all us cottage mercantilists know the drill that follows. You seat the man to his task, you clasp his shoulder firmly and then you give it three gentle pats. The first action is to suggest that a dropped decimal point'll reap him at least three horribly strangled loved ones. The second indicates a bit of "my-fate-is-in-your-hands" grovelling. Then you back out of the room, quietly and respectfully, leaving him with five grocery bags stuffed full of receipts and a well-oiled pencil sharpener handy.

Outside the ops room the coffee pot is already stoked with enough grounds to made an EPA pilot's eyes smart. Every other appliance is unplugged to give his adding machine full wattage. The deductions are sleeping soundly under the influence of gripe water and straight gin. You sit there bolt upright for hours, gazing at the closed door. You spring to attention when, from time to time, it opens. You maintain the coffee relay, you let slide a claim for 5,000 paper clips, you defend two orders of fish and chips as reciprocal entertainment. Finally, the waiting ends. He opens the door slowly, he shakes his head. The voice comes as if from a great distance. "There are various nasty little plateaus, you see, all along the route. They're the constant bane of amateurs. When you slip over one of them some rather alarming things can happen ... in your case, a $3,007.67 underpayment."

Before the hour was out, I saw my spouse transformed from a lifelong flaming pinko into a roaring rightwinger. It was an awesome spectacle. The civil service was to be slaughtered right down to the janitorial level and pensioners reduced to stewing their domestic pets. I tried to comfort the household as best I could with what was left of the children's gripe water and some Newfoundland fatalism. "Let us thank God for small mercies, my dears," I said as I stowed the accountant's used coffee grounds away in a Baggie for a special treat next Christmas. "If the past fiscal year hadn't been so disastrous for us, we'd have ended up in the poorhouse."

You don't have to batter me more than once with nasty little tax plateaus before I commence to get the hang of it. "It was heavensent," I consoled the little brood, "when that mainland magazine went belly-up still owing me for two pieces; providence smiled when that Toronto journal evaporated before I could collect expenses; roses bloomed when I fell an ignorant victim to those book publishers. What a stroke of fortune when the CBC's budget was clipped by $81 million and the very first crusts of bread the Corp. snatched were from Chez Guy; it's thanks to a merciful Creator that a rural weekly stuck me for the making of two car payments and nothing less than Hibernian luck when, for mother's sake, I turned down that beer commercial."

This optimistic litany worked wonders. We were soon dancing ring-around-the-rosie and laying happy plans for bankruptcy next year. My spouse had now decided she was a Chrysler socialist. A few days later the tax accountant sent me a dry cleaning bill. He'll wait until either hell or my assets freeze and there's no doubt in my own mind which will occur first.

PEACE, GOOD WIFE. WE MAY ENTERTAIN ANGELS UNAWARE

In a square in the city of London there may sometimes be seen a huge mechanical monster. The thing has a human form but it looks loathsome, ugly, barbaric. It is supposed to be us.

Schoolchildren are led by the hand to it to hiss and spit and scream degradation at us.

Animal-loving zealots and penny-catching frauds have discovered modern pressure techniques. Their brush is broad and their paint as black as smut. Such immoral propaganda blackens not just sealhunters but certainly all Newfoundlanders, all the people of Atlantic Canada, all Canadians.

What else might the English child who sees that hideous effigy know of us? Canadians who support this extremism should reconsider the balance between their goals and the damage they do their country. The balance between free speech and treason.

Modern communications are such that the images of peoples, politicians, countries are often boiled down to 25 words or less. Until those "jokes" came along, Newfoundland was known by only three ... Smallwood, fog and screech. And that in many parts of Canada itself.

Newfie jokes, anti-sealing extremism ... the effect of both is cumulative. At first, those jokes seemed like harmless little jabs. We persuaded ourselves that we were big enough to take them but they built up intolerably.

Pretty soon if you mentioned your birthplace abroad you were like as not to get, "Yuck, yuck, yuck, did you leave your other head at home?"

It seemed that our turn to be ridiculed had come round. Before us there were the Irish, the Jews, the Blacks, the Poles and others. The hurtful part was that many of the people who heard and repeated the damned things knew nothing else of Newfoundland or Newfoundlanders.

At their height, I got snickers at the mere mention of Newfoundland in places as far apart as Barbados and Vancouver.

Once a simplistic image of a place or people gets set in the minds of mean people, the devil himself wouldn't budge it. Hence the persistent slanders that the Irish are lazy, Italians are cowardly, Poles are dumb, Jews are money-grubbing, Roman Catholics are priest-ridden, Newfies are goofy.

However, for the sake of our ancestors and our children (and the children of others who are being taught to hate and revile us) we've got a duty to batter away against the lies and the bigotry.

I will speak of my own folk and of Newfoundland, not to boast or to set them above others, but because they're examples I know best.

There is much goodness and kindness in Newfoundland. And wisdom and gentle simplicity, hospitality and love of others. No more than elsewhere perhaps, but, God witnessing, no less.

Newfoundlanders have a tender, sentimental, almost maudlin streak. Grown men sometimes weep like faucets in public … and not only in their beer, boyo. I remember the cracker barrel brigade in our small shop dabbing their eyes and moaning softly as Mr. Auerbach told his stories. He was in wholesale and Father would get him to show his tattoo and tell about the concentration camps.

At a Holocaust Remembrance this April, Moshe Kantorowitz told his audience that he is grateful for finding "peace, tolerance and tranquillity in Newfoundland."

Oh, there has been religious bigotry here, plenty of it. It was brought over, all of a piece, from the old country. But the bright part is, it has now all but perished … in a place where, perhaps life was too hard, too sweet, too short to waste in the hatred of your neighbour.

I can't think of another single thing — with the ancient hatreds, sadness and wars still flaring evilly in the places of our origins — that is more to the glory and honour of my province.

There are those who say we haven't been tested and they may be right. Fresh immigration has been tiny so far; we're still 95 per cent Irish and English stock. We can only wait in hope and in resolve.

There has always been much poverty here. But even in the days when a year's income might be less than $100, the missionary boxes didn't go away from us empty. I remember Grandma Guy telling us children that the stockings she was knitting were "for them poor little nigger boys and girls over there in foreign parts."

She put as much time and care into those as she did into things for her grandchildren ... and this was typical of everyone.

My Grandpa Adams revelled in hospitality and charity in the high Victorian style. He would collar as many of the strangers, wayfarers and the needy as came to his door and have them in. Once when provisions were perilously low, Grandma warned him and he is said to have replied with a fine Shakespearian flourish: "Peace, good wife. We may entertain angels, unaware."

I warned you there was a maudlin streak hereabouts. But I have a silly fantasy that, if we ever do come into our own, the Lieutenant Governor would declare and say: "In the name of God and for the help of our sister, India, Newfoundland gives one zillion dollars" ... or at least the equivalent of those stockings way back then.

A more recent besmirchment to our escutcheon is that we're greedy, grab-all and selfish. The gas and oil squabble kicked that one off. Yet look how kind we are to let our dear neighbour, Québec, take hundreds of millions from Churchill Falls reserving less than $10 million to ourselves.

Never fear. We have always been suckers for every sob-story and carpetbagger to come down the turnpike. If we ever do get one cent to rub against another out of this oil racket then, sure, there'll be the merriest shindig ever seen in these waters for life is all too short ... but there'll be lots for others. Not that we have to buy our friends or our dignity.

All that being said, the problem of how to save those English children — and others in parts both foreign and domestic — from that nightmarish image of us remains.

Perhaps there's a way to get a message to them of things that are really true. Of things as in Cassie Brown's book Death on the Ice. Where men — yes, sealers — who had a bit more strength left than their sons, brothers, friends, lay upon them and beside them to give them the heat of their bodies until the last sparks went out of their own.

We know who it was who said there was love no greater.

So, to all children and as always, from Newfoundland, with love.

OF FAMILY AND FRIENDS

THERE'S NO REFUGE ANYWHERE FROM DIABOLICAL FADS

S orry," said the clerk at K-Mart, "but we haven't got one character lunch box left."

I hadn't asked for a character lunch box or a lunch box of character. Didn't know what a character lunch box was. But it was school-opening time, the salespersons had seen our two youngsters trailing behind me and knew it was character lunch boxes or nothing.

No self-respecting child would resume the march toward greater knowledge without "Mr. T." or some "Smurfs" or Michael Jackson on the side of its dinner pail.

Its parents wouldn't be caught without someone else's name... Calvin Klein or Gloria Vanderbilt...stamped across their backsides, so why should these innocent cherubs be deprived?

"Character" underdrawers and lunch boxes and various and sundry are nothing new. Did not the original Teddy Bear have connections to President Theodore Roosevelt and isn't the Mickey Mouse watch almost an antique? I went to school in an aviator cap looking like a dwarf "Lucky Lindy", and to church during World War II in a sailor suit, a direct challenge to the Hun.

What's different now is the constant stream of these gadgets and the ferocity with which parents and kinder alike go after them.

Those who were there say the great Hong Kong bank crash had nothing on Cabbage Patch door openings. People trample each other to get one of the brutes. I notice that Superman, of all people, strikes out against the immorality of it all in his recent daily comic strips.

The Man of Steel is a fine one to talk...although I wouldn't tug on his cape and tell him to his face. He suckered me into one of his kryptonite code rings when I was still in knee pants. It's like *Playboy* disparaging *Penthouse* for those snaps of the former Miss America.

What else is different (at least in Newfoundland) is the speed with which these fads reach us now.

We had to wait nearly a year for a Davy Crockett coonskin cap. Later, it took hula hoops six months or more to reach these shores. Now, *Ghostbusters* is on the screen almost before the *Time* magazine review arrives.

Before TV, the mail-order catalogues whipped up the demand. Eaton's and Simpson's instilled covetousness into our black little hearts. Christmas was shot to hell if there wasn't a Barbara Ann Scott dolly under the tree or a "Punkinhead" teddy in the stocking.

One year the catalogues ganged up and brought forth something of a miracle among us pubertal bucks. It rigged us out in flaming pink. Both Simpson's and Eaton's decreed that charcoal black and searing pink were the colours for anyone reeking of brylcreem and we took it down, hook, line and sinker.

It's television, though, that whips today's tiny tots into froth of lusty consumption. If I never see a bloody Smurf again for as long as I live I won't be too heartbroken. Mister T and Michael Jackson can jump each other into slushy puddles and I won't lie awake chewing the sheets.

But, gag me with a Care Bear, the most diabolical contraption of all time is that thing sometimes known as the "ghetto blaster." When the transistor radio first came in, I signed a petition to reopen hostilities against Japan. Yet they were as baby poops to elephant flatulence compared to the latest earhole crucifiers.

Big as weekend suitcases with dinnerplate speakers spewing aural cyanide, these are loud enough to blast twigs off the trees and make their owners' blackheads pulsate. It should be legal to chuck rocks at them.

Trends reach Newfoundland almost immediately these days, but a small, isolated city like St. John's sometimes finds the burden a weighty one to bear.

Bars, for instance. Fern, macho, wine, gay, piano, bistro — they're all here but for want of custom, two or more "themes" have to be combined in one. You could be tickled by both the ferns and the patrons in a single hootchery.

Quiche has been here and has just about had it, but phasing it out for a shot at the sushi is a chancy business. Jello wrestling had its day, but when Miss K-9 and her Great Dane arrived from Montreal to fill the void, the pious element in the city denied her access.

Windsurfers are few and far between; there used to be a mechanical bull, but it's long since shot its nuts and bolts; fake crab landed this summer, but the package tasted better.

Video arcades rose and fell. Video tapes are now the rage, but several outlets have been pounced on for pornography. Miss K-9 of Montreal tried to get in the back way.

It's also a small and isolated population that counters trends here. Ersatz punks, let us say, easily blend in with all the other curios on Yonge Street. In St. John's they'd merely be taken for baymen, which ruins the whole point of it.

On the other hand, I recently heard of the case of a large woman from, let us say, Kumquat Quay, home on furlough from Camp Gagetown. She was dickied up in full leathers, spiked orange hair and a safety pin through her cheek. That took guts, you may think, but her reception in the village was remarkable.

Her dear old dad boasted pridefully that she would frighten the spit out of any Rooshian yet born, and her granny laughed so hard she had to be sedated.

It's still the middle-class trends that find fertile soil in this neck of the woods. Last year, for instance, three parts of the womenfolk dressed in a grubby sort of purple, about the shade of a black eye on the fourth day. At the decree of the catalogues and the chain stores, they perambulate this year in a gruesome combination of magenta and turquoise.

This is not to say we have no couth. This summer, *Esquire* told us that the "in" tipple in the States was the Mimosa, a mix of orange juice and champagne. No sooner said than I saw it on the menu of a downtown hash house alongside the grilled cheese and the hot turkey sandwiches.

But back to the kiddies' corner. Our two primary scholars set off to school with plain-old generic lunch boxes, their own names written on the sides. I was sure they'd be mocked, jeered and perhaps set upon, so I gave them a quick course in defence — which part of their assailant, according to gender, to put the boots to, and all that.

No such thing. When I collected them that day they were much enthused and greatly impressed with daddy's eye for fashion. Their unique lunch buckets were widely admired and some of their little pals begged to know where they could be had.

Well, like gag me with a Smurfette, have I started another fad?

WHY CHILDREN SHOULD BE SEEN AND NOT HEARD

A bullet hole through the cap was all the rage with us one summer, I recall. You stuck your cap on a post and drilled it from ear to ear with a .22 at close range so as to have the benefit of the powder burn, too. This was after sculpin funerals palled and sometime before we nearly snuffed poor old Mr. Parsons with a Molotov cocktail.

Our youthful amusements in those days were simple and robust. Except for a few "Windchargers" there was no electricity. The radio battery had to be spared along for the news.

Guns were in astonishing profusion and discharged all over the place with suicidal abandon. Most homes had three or four...a shotgun, a .22 and a .303 rifle or so. Their legitimate use was for moose, caribou and game birds but most lads could sneak them out of the house whenever the fancy moved.

They were in great demand at weddings. The thing here was to put an extra heavy load in a .12-gauge shotgun and try to knock bits out of the eaves on the church porch just as the happy couple emerged. Before one of these nuptial volleys, one of our number fell heavily into some purloined homebrew and discharged his piece through the window just as the parson was asking if there was any just cause why Emmy Lou and Arthur Wilberforce Isaiah should not be spliced.

This pitched one of the bridesmaids into hysterics and the clergy roared out the door after us like the Archangel Michael with a seizure.

It was said to be the greatest blasphemy since the time, some years before, when a cow had somehow been hoisted up inside the belfry and burst forth in bovine terror during the reading of the Second Lesson.

But we were by no means anti-religion. We took sculpin funerals quite seriously. A sculpin (for the benefit of farmers among us) is possibly the ugliest fish in creation, three-parts head and mouth and bristling with spikes. Once you catch one, a proper burial seems to be the only decent thing.

We gave our sculpins the full Church of England treatment with some elements of Salvation Army chucked in for good measure. The Established Church was represented by a chappie in a bedsheet while the Sally Ann "officer" whanged the bejazus out of a bread pan and played the mouth organ at the same time.

I'd read about Molotov cocktails in a book. As luck should have it, one of my tasks was to retail kerosene and gas from barrels kept in a small shed on the edge of a 40-foot cliff.

When the coast was clear, the lads would gather behind the shed with a few bottles and rags and we'd hurl the bombs to the beach below and the flash and the roar of the explosions were lovely indeed.

It was arms escalation that nearly did in poor old Mr. Parsons. He was deeply religious and wonderfully absentminded. He used to shuffle around all over the place looking down at the ground and singing hymns. This particular evening we were particularly ambitious and filled a gallon rum jar with naptha gasoline.

Just as we flung this blockbuster to the beach below, poor old Mr. Parsons came out from behind a rock singing loudly to himself about, if memory serves, "The Sweet Bye and Bye".

Heaven and hell came together with a dreadful boom and pillar of fire not 20 feet away from his toes. His reaction was remarkable. He looked up with the most beatific expression on his face and continued on his way singing louder than ever. Saul on the road to Damascus now had a modern counterpart.

After dark in fair weather we went "skimming." This interesting enterprise involved stalking courting couples in the age group ahead of us and pelting them with mud balls and similar as soon as they got wrapped up in their unspeakable practices. One enraged swain tore after us and gave chase for more than a mile — in his bare feet on a gravel road, naked as a jay bird.

A favourite trysting place was a net loft belonging to the father of one of our number. You could climb a ladder outside and peep in through knotholes. He felt justified in charging us an admission of five cents per head and double that if it was his sister and her beau getting down to cases inside.

Most of us chose to boycott his higher rates and spend the dime on a cream soda or a bag of chips instead.

Interference with livestock was also a great juvenile pastime. Catching ponies for a bareback ride, milking goats into a tin can, lofting cats on kites. Nothing, however, beat sheep.

Nearly every family in the village kept a dozen or more sheep. You had only to catch one, attach a tin can to its tail and it drew the entire mutton population to it like a magnet. It created a woolly stampede, a snowballing effect, a growing avalanche that swept through the roads and lanes capsizing baby carriages into ditches and driving old age pensioners up the sides of fences.

On a routine basis, the law was threatened on us. Pieces of paper were waved at us which were claimed to be telegrams to the magistrate. We figured he must be up to the hips in the transgressions of his own bailiwick because he never did show up.

Mostly, you just got roared and bawled at. Some of the women had prodigious lung power and in top form on a calm day could be heard a half a mile away. We would try to drown out this litany in case our parents overheard by singing as loudly as possible, "I lost me arm in the army..." or some other childhood ditty.

Two or three of the older male residents, though, were gratifyingly easy to send round the twist. They'd pop their corks at the slightest provocation. You had only to sidle up while they were harnessing their horses, let us say, and dab some Sloane's linament under the creatures' tails and they'd fly into a homicidal rage.

The best part about it was, they brought you along to your own door by the ear so often and were in such a frantic emotional state that your parents soon got bored with them and would give them little or no credit.

These jolly old grouches took top priority whenever there was a handful of firecrackers to be chucked down a chimney after the doorstep had been moved to one side.

We got away with a lot but when a true bill of indictment was brought against us the medicine handed out would have warmed the cockles of Robespierre.

Strangely, though, whenever our dear old dads loosened up and talked about their own boyhood pranks they made ours sound down right sissy.

Surely, at that rate, few if any of them would have escaped the gallows unless they tended to exaggerate as the years went by.

That is certainly not the case here — cross my heart and soap your windows.

THE HAZARDS OF CATS, KIDS AND SQUISHY PUSSY-TREET

I took to cats long before I could walk. I think many infants do. When you're crawling around the floor you can't see much more than Teddy, adult ankles and cats.

There are always adults around, clumping about, but you can't see their heads on top of their shoulders ... just as when you move close to a column and can't see the statue on top.

Adults can be rather scary. Consider. Suppose you're lying on the carpet reading this tasteful organ and, suddenly, you are grabbed and swooped up into the air, 20 feet high or more.

A huge red face with teeth is thrust up against yours. The giant's breath is hot and it makes growling idiot noises and cluck clucks at you. You'd probably grab its eyeglasses and pee all over it, too.

But cats are no bigger than Teddy. Cats are soft. Cats make low purring noises.

After I left home I was catless for many a long year. The hiatus ended when at last I entered into Holy Acrimony. Now, at time of writing, I have one spouse, two youngsters and three of the finest cats you'd ever wish to clap eyes on.

The principal of the trio is Cecil. He was brought home to commemorate the visit, six years ago, of the Queen. Cecil — because have not the ancient line of Cecils served the Crown long and well?

When we got him from the animal shelter he wasn't much to look at. But the stamp of the destiny was upon him. In full fighting trim he weighs 22 3/4 pounds and meter readers and delivery persons seldom fail to exclaim: "God in Heaven! What's *that*?"

Cecil doesn't do much. Blood sports interest him not at all. This may be because mice look to him like sow bugs and sparrows like houseflies.

I've promised him a live turkey on his next birthday in an effort to bring some interest and challenge into his life.

Because of his bulk, the Great One can manage to hurl himself on to the sofa only if he can get at least a 20-foot run, or, in his case, waddle.

At feeding time, most cats tend to bump against your legs. When Cecil bumps, so may you. Once when he got me good I ended on the floor with one hand in a dish of squishy Pussy-Treet "saveur de thon" and doubts that I'd ever walk again, roaring at the youngsters to stop their snickering or brief life would be their portion.

Second in line comes Turpin. He is the most villainous-looking thing on four legs that I have ever seen. In a beauty contest with a wolverine and a Tasmanian devil he'd come third.

Turpin (for Dick Turpin, the highwayman) looks like he should have a cutlass between his teeth and a patch on one eye.

There's a running battle between him and our younger child. It never fails. Anne is proceeding carefully down the hall with her bread and jam and glass of milk. Turpin waits till she's past then flings himself at her ankle, bunny-kicking furiously with his hind feet.

For her part, Anne can't pass Turpin if he's lying there in twitchy sleep without bringing her little fist smartly down upon the top of his head. He springs awake with a bowel-melting glare. Next reincarnation, he's coming back as a Bengal tiger and you can bet he knows whom he'll be shredding first.

Turpin, also known as "Rough Trade," is constantly pouncing on Cecil and on his sister with what sometimes seems to be lascivious intent.

Since we'd paid the vet good money to circumvent Nature, I asked the doctor about this. He allowed as there might be "some residual testicular matter."

Bring Turpin in again, he said, and he'd have another whack at him. No siree bob, said I and walked out the door with rather mincing steps. Is not empathy one of the finer virtues?

Although he looks like Bluebeard after a hard six months of looting and pillaging, Turpin fancies himself. Whenever two or three humans are gathered together, he carefully grooms his pantaloons and mustachios and parades up and down like an 18th century French fop on a fashion show runway.

Penny is Penny because she's the colour of one. She's a neat, compact little creature with only half a mew ... a barely audible squeak. And she's one of the most deadly killers imaginable.

The carnage is especially brisk in early summer among birds that are slow on takeoff, and in the fall when the field mice are moving to winter quarters.

Cats make Lucretia Borgia look like Mother Teresa. When they catch something they merely cripple it. Then they'll play with it for an hour and when it finally croaks they take it as a personal affront.

On Sunday mornings in summer, Penny is sure to drag something fluttering and screeching directly below the bedroom window. Starlings are the most terrible screechers of all. I have to shuffle out in my bathrobe and finish off the poor brutes with a large wooden spoon.

Penny, the Half-a-Mew, keeps much to herself, but one day Anne decided Penny had the flu and should be put to bed.

Anne has a remarkably high pain threshold and the determination of a salmon headed upstream. James Bond would crack under interrogation and deliver the House of Windsor to the KGB before Annie would say what happened to that whole package of fig bars.

She'd been trying, perhaps for 15 minutes, to get dolly's flannel nightie on Penny. The struggle was ferocious but nearly silent. By the time the fray was discovered, the nightie was in shreds and so was Anne — just this side of needing a transfusion.

These are our cats now but there've been others.

I remember Hodge. He was as small and scrawny as the young Sinatra and had bat ears like the Prince of Wales. He was named after Dr. Samuel Johnson's pet whose master went out to fetch oysters for pussy's dish himself lest the servant be irked by the chore and mistreat the cat.

Hodge never enjoyed good health. The vet gave us something called "bitch's supplement." It's used to build up dogs after they've pupped, but the doctor figured it might help cats, too.

My mother-in-law had just come to visit. That morning from the kitchen I called out to my wife: "Precieuse! Have you made up the bitch's supplement, yet?"

M.-in-Law claims she thought she was about to get her breakfast in bed.

Cats pretty much please themselves. They don't slobber all over you like dogs. They're selfish, cruel, destructive and snooty.

Not lovable creatures at all, really. Yet why does your throat ache so much on that final trip to the vet? Or why do you keep watch for weeks when they sometimes go out the door and never come back?

FEBRUARY FLOWERS THAT BLOOM IN THE MIND, UNTOUCHED BY DIRT

February is a favourite gardening month with many of us keen amateurs.

With snowplows fighting a losing battle, the rake and shovel safely rusting away in the shed and all threat of digging and delving still months away, we can wallow in horticultural theory and trivia without the wear and tear of practice.

Such questions as, "Should granny have been hove in the clink?" come as easily and as idly as a fresh hot toddy.

Well, granny *did* grow opium poppies, didn't she? Mine did. Each year she produced a booming crop of that self-same *Papaver somniferum*, source of morphine, opium and heroin, cause of revolutions in China and crime waves in New York.

Granny's opium poppies reseeded themselves each year and sprouted among the Sweet William, bouncing bet and cranesbill — and the constables admired them in passing.

These days, our maggotty-headed young layabouts are collared for growing marijuana, for gathering magic mushrooms — even the seeds of the Heavenly Blue morning glory, said to contain a mild equivalent to LSD, are coated with a vile, nasty-tasting substance to foil the rascals.

But where stands the law on the growing of opium poppies? If I mistake not, the seeds are readily available from some seed houses and in the spice sections of our supermarkets. Passing strange, by Gad. (February horticultural theorists tend to say things like "by Gad." And it doesn't hurt, either, to affect a crooked stem pipe and have an arthritic Labrador retriever twitching in front of the grate.)

Enter the memsahib with her back copy of *Country Life* and you wonder aloud how it came about that Newfoundland has a meat eater as its floral emblem.

The pitcher plant, as it's called nowadays, but in my time, known as Indian pipes, grows on bogs and digests insects and perhaps the occasional tadpole or nestling bird. It's a floral emblem that inspires confidence. I'd stack it against a trillium in the ring any day.

Ah, what a lovely scent from the fireplace. How many thousands of years old are the plants in that peat? Newfoundland has at last begun to use its bogs for burning so that we can say with the Irishman, "Other countries may be going down the drain but, shure, we do be sending ours up the chimney."

Now is the time of year to polish your Latin plant names. It makes a nice impression if, come summer in Ottawa you can poke your blackthorn into a batch of leaves and say: "By Gad, Madame, a finer stand of *Zantendeschia aethiopica* I have not seen in a dog's age." Yes, most Governors General are tickled when you admire their calla lilies in Latin.

For all that, "Jesus flannel" or "lambs ears" as we used to call it does more than *Stachys lanata* to evoke those old cottage gardens on the lids of shortbread boxes. So do granny's bonnets (*aquilegias*) or the deep blue *Geranium phaeum* known to us as mourning widow or little niggers.

Right now, if you're lucky, the hydro lines will snap so that you can light up a kerosene lamp or two. That mellow glow nicely underlines winter in the higher latitudes. Small wonder that even ten years ago, the Norwegians purchased 14 million houseplants on an average of ten per household.

Hummm, did that whimper come from Lab or from the memsahib? Small matter. If you've got hold of all this horticultural trivia, when else are you going to discharge it if not in the midst of a February blizzard?

"Everything that grew out of the mould was healing herb to our fathers of old." Strange but one can't seem to recollect many of the local countryman's old remedies. Maybe they've been washed away on a tide of senna tea and castor oil.

But most houses kept a mixture made from what we called "beaver root," the yellow pond lily; a salve for horses was made from the ground yew and cuts were stuck together with blisters from the balsam fir.

Did you know we still call the balsam fir the "snotty var" after the old usage of Cornwall?

Interesting stuff, plant lore. The peony root, so prized as a medicine by the ancient Romans, had a kingfisher to guard it. Or was that the mandrake? At any rate, the peony screamed when torn from the ground which was certain death to all who heard it.

So the clever Romans tied a stout dog to the plant, stood back a safe distance with their ears stopped and waved around a porkchop which fetched the dog along, the root in tow.

Was it Sydney who said: "doubtless, God could have made a better berry but, doubtless, God never did." The strawberry was, of course, known to both Virgil and Pliny the Elder but not in its present form. Oh, no. Not until shortly before 1800 was there that happy marriage between *Fragaria virginiana* and the Chilean berry, *F. chiloensis*, which had been taken to France by Captain Frezier in 1712 ...

Merciful heaven, did that low growl come from the Lab or was it really the memsahib? Horticultural trivia is not to every taste. Little do such persons know that an infusion of the root of *Valeriana officinalis* is certain cure for ragged nerves.

Quite so, an interesting plant, the valerian. It affects cats as catnip does — and is also attractive to rats!

Did you know that the Pied Piper of Hamelin had valerian roots in his pocket when he led the rats into the river? Now you do. And that in cases of hypochondria, hysteria, epilepsy, migraine, nervous upsets, croup bruises, coughs and the plague, valerian was once thought to be at least as efficacious as running your head into a brick wall.

And strange, isn't it, about the political connections of plants. In Scotland, they call Sweet William "reeking billy" out of disaffection for William, Duke of Cumberland, "the butcher" of Culloden; and "Monsieur Violette ..." none other than N. Bonaparte who promised to return with the violets; and the orange lily which blooms in Ulster on or about "The Glorious Twelfth" and the ...

By Gad! Damme, if that brute of a Lab hasn't sunk its fangs right through one's plus fours and the memsahib, for some strange reason, has picked up the poker. Toodle-doo.

DOWN WITH DISHWASHERS. UP WITH USEFUL GADGETS

A aaoow, a dishwasher!" crooned one's spouse in rapture and within earshot of the real estate salesman. I knew the game was lost.

"But, adorable," I countered weakly, "have you seen the back view ... there's a lovely vista of the exercise yard for the criminally insane."

"A-dish-wash-er", she said, low and slow and in a semi-trance, very like the ecstasy of St. Theresa in which an angel with a flaming golden arrow pierced her heart repeatedly.

"As recently as the fall of 1978," I said, "if memory serves, a migration of 4,000 rats was seen coming up from the Waterford River through that very field ..."

Of course, we bought the dishwasher complete with a house attached. Don't get me wrong. I'm a greater gadget freak than most, specializing in useless and non inexpensive gadgets. Item: An induction balance, multi-coil, water-immersible treasure finder with which I have so far recovered three coppers, 35 pounds of old tire chains and two bushels of beer bottle stoppers.

Item: a camera of the very type used to capture the Princess of Wales in the throes of morning sickness (and other international disasters) and with which I chop off the heads of the youngsters twice a year, at Christmas and on birthdays.

Item: electrical carpentry tools; others have used less to whip together country estates, yet my construction of a bird feeder has now entered its third year with tremendous cost overrun.

Gadgets yes. But there comes the point — don't you think? — when gadgetry leaves the realm of ridiculous self indulgence and slops over into the absurd. Dishwashers, for instance.

First crack out of the box, let me bung a cork into charges of "male chauvinist pig" and other feminist piffle. In pre-dishwasher days I took my fair trick and turn at the sink. My talented though stubby digits are still soft, pale and wrinkled like two bunches of subterranean grubs.

Did I ever complain? Not a bit of it! There's something so elemental and satisfying about washing dishes. Sudsy water just at the pain threshold; the sunlight fracturing on one's container of detergent, turning it into a huge globular jewel of green, pink or yellow; Peter Gzowski, warm and reassuring as a teddy bear, murmuring hope and enlightenment to the housepersons of the nation.

During these idyllic moments, up to my elbows in the sink, my thoughts would turn to Sophia Loren. Once on the late, late show in a medieval farce, Sophia emerged victorious in a dishwashing contest for the hand of a princely nerd. Low cut and bent over a huge vat of steaming water, she achieved a certain sublime poetry of motion, turning slightly from side to side from the waist, dipping and stacking, dipping and stacking, dipping and sta ... pausing only to brush a lank lock of hair from eyes that would sear the sun or to wipe her nose, peasant fashion, on the back of her hand.

Baroque as was my attitude to washing dishes in the sink, I entered the Age of Reason when it came to drying them. That is to say, with cool Scandinavian logic I cracked open the kitchen window and left the air to do it ... no lint, no squeaks, no sweat, no breakage.

With a dishwashing machine you do not find yourself drifting into reveries to do with Sophia Loren. R2-D2, is more like it. It is neither a sensual nor a logical enterprise. Scrape the plates, knock the crud out of the pots. Fiddle and rattle the crockery into these infernally complicated wire baskets. Stab your wrists on the up-pointing knives. Shake in the acrid powder with the skeletal hand and the skull and crossbones on the package. Poke the buttons. Then comes the monstrous commotion, the squelch, the floosh and the gurgle, like half a tribe of over-ripe Celts coursing through the viscera of Gog and Magog.

Rude noises, miserable noises, ominous noises. There's the steady *whish, whish, whish* like the sound in your head when you've a filthy fever. Or the heart-stopping Gatling gun when a piece of wedding sterling gets meshed in the works. Let us turn our faces aside from unloading and stowing away.

Dishwashers are mild stuff compared to what's facing us. Next year we'll be in the throes of talking cars. "Sod the humping levy," your Chevy will snap at you. "It's still in a dry mode, parameter-wise you breeding runatic ..." its voice box having been slung together by mad scientists from the U.S., the U.K. and Japan.

Ban the cruise missile and shower the Ruskies with talking cars. That would soon have them howling for the dear old Romanovs. Here's Vassily tooling down to the dacha, the former hammer throw champion of Minsk by his side, and, suddenly, his car starts to give him all manner of lip and abuse for squashing a Rhodeillyavitch Island Red, hero egg layer at glorious peoples commune 782, and punches up the tape of his night in a hotel room in Smolensk with the student ballerina, Comrade Svetlana Tugoff.

The very fibre of Soviet family life would thus be soaked to a mush by the cream of democratic technology.

Paranoia is leading us up still another path of absurd gadgetry. Pity the second-storey man with the weak ticker. He has but to think of jimmying a window and all the devils in hell break loose around his head — flashing floodlights, earsplitting sirens, alarms going off at police and fire HQs, taped killer Alsatians, the neighbourhood militia, tear gas shooting out the arrow slits, tell-tale ink pouring down from the ramparts.

Ridiculous excess, it seems to me. Thousands squandered on protective gadgets when nothing is more discouraging — some of my more enterprising though unlucky relatives inform me — than a smart tap along kneecaps with a softball bat.

Household computers and word processors are already a raging current against which sensible persons such as ourselves cannot hope to sail. Yet let us raise a squeak even as we are being plowed under. It is nonsense to pay $5,000 for a machine that will advise you to crunch Taxation Canada's next demand for $3,822 into a neat ball and pitch it in the trash. Even if it also gets the coffee pot going at 7:20 a.m. precisely.

Word processors??? How, pray tell, does such a gadget process words? Do you fit it with the chopping blade, plug it in, add half a cup of mucilage, toss in the *Shorter Oxford English Dictionary* and end up with a poem by William Blake plastered across the kitchen ceiling? Go away with you, boy. Don't be so foolish.

To return to dishwashing machines. What I will do — when I get my chance — is sell it second-hand. The proceeds I will put toward a new improved up-market model of an induction balance, multi-coil, water-immersible treasure finder.

That charitable fund-raising plea to allow 15 Pentacostals to emigrate from Moncton will just have to wait.

A CHRISTMAS LAMENT FOR
A CHILD'S LOSS OF FAITH

It's Baby Jesus time again and a cruel annual reminder to a Bad Daddy such as myself that it is only for the lack of millstones in these parts that I haven't been drowned in the depths of the sea. That's the stern medicine set down in Scriptures for those who offend little ones: A millstone necklace and a boot over the gunwales above the Mariana Trench. My offence against the throne of heavenly grace is that I knocked our five-year-old completely off her prayers two years ago. She's got her little heels stuck firmly in against even the "Now-I-Lay-Me-Downs." Should she die before she wakes, she is not concerned in the slightest about the deposition of her soul.

Theology and the little ones, of course, are an extremely delicate mixture. Try as you will, they persist in squirreling away their punch-out Easter Bunnies in the spring to stick behind the punch-out cardboard manger scenes at Christmas. Not quite cricket for one baptised in the established Church.

Should my first offspring's feet be directed at some time in the future toward a Jonestown instead of Canterbury, the blame would lie heavily on me. What is a Bad Daddy to do? Pass her over to the Jesuits until she is eight?

A Bad Daddy thinks not. He chooses, instead, to put it all down on paper here so that she may cut it out and save it and not have to go to the uncertain extreme of dashing off a letter to Ann Landers when in her teens. By that time, she would have to blow her dowry on the postage stamp, anyway.

It was her Bad Daddy's high-stomached pride that set his oldest daughter's mind against the Baby Jesus.

I had a cat which I named "Hodge." That was an outrageous thing to do. There is a superstition in Newfoundland that boats' names are not to be tampered with, and I think now it must also apply to those of feline pets. Dr. Samuel Johnson thought so highly of his cat, Hodge, that he perambulated down to the fishmonger's himself to get it a few dozen oysters rather than send his servant, lest that irksome chore turn said servant's mind against the brute to the extent that he would then mistreat it.

If you follow. My Hodge got squashed in a neighbour's driveway. Well, perhaps not squashed first. I think he expired due to natural causes and then got squashed a little. In any case he went to pussy-cat heaven.

Trouble is, our older child was told that Hodge had gone to live with Baby Jesus. So finely tuned is her sense of property that for the two years past she has not forgiven the aforementioned Infant. By what right did Baby Jesus take away daddy's Hodge, her Hodge. She remains unconsoled. How, then, do you explain to a five-year-old that in Newfoundland the majority of the people are accustomed to speaking directly and distinctly to God?

Or that her father was once on an extremely small boat in an extremely heavy gale when the extremely simple engine conked and there was an extremely good chance of death among the hardest rocks and the wettest water in the world. And that, then, the captain of the boat said, "Very well then, damn You to hell's flames, God. I have kept up my end of the bargain. What about Yours?"

With that, the engine started. Which says lots — as I have indeed told my oldest daughter — for plain speech, and for extremely simple engines, and for being God-fearing without wetting your pants when coming face to face with said Party. But do you think she'll say her prayers?

I and Baby Jesus try to get in the back way. She knows and her sister knows, too, that bunny rabbits and fields of corn don't go together. She'll soon reply to me that the season is too short in Newfoundland for corn and that we don't have rabbits, we have arctic hares, and so the problem remains. But still she sings:

Root them out, get them gone All the little bunnies in the fields of corn Envy, hatred, malice, pride These shall never in my heart abide.

It is small encouragement. Another Nativity has rolled round and a miserable little cat named Hodge is still gone. Baby Jesus has still got him. Hodge has bat ears and is extremely scrawny.

Due to his absence — pay strict attention, God — You suffer the loss of one child's prayers. So, clean up Your act, Old Man. You know and I know that Hodge went to the Robin Hood Bay dump in the Glad bag and that I'm not so good at explaining these things. But You did hear me say at the time, didn't you, "God help me," and You didn't.

Anyway, I forgive You. You have your troubles, God knows. But if Your 2,000-year-old offspring and my five-year-old offspring aren't on better terms next year I shall really have my doubts.

Happy Birthday to the little Fellow from me in any case.